Behavioral Science &
Policy Association

december 2015
vol. 1, no. 2

Craig R. Fox
Sim B. Sitkin
Editors

Behavioral Science & Policy is a publication of the Behavioral Science & Policy Association,
P.O. Box 51336, Durham, NC 27717-1336, and is published twice yearly with the Brookings
Institution, 1775 Massachusetts Avenue, NW, Washington, DC 20036, and through the
Brookings Institution Press.

To order a journal subscription, please go to: https://behavioralpolicy.org/signup/#subscribe
Please note that subscriptions are entered on a calendar year basis (January–December) and
expire with the last issue of the last volume listed.

The journal may be accessed through Project Muse (http://muse/jhu.edu).

table of contents

december 2015 vol. 1, no. 2

editors' note

Welcome to the second issue of *Behavioral Science & Policy* (*BSP*). We are pleased to present eight articles that extend the reach of behavioral science research across a wide range of policy applications. Some articles focus on everyday individual activities such as debt repayment and paying government vehicle fees online. Others examine ambitious social policy objectives such as strengthening families and reducing bias in criminal justice systems. Still others speak to global challenges such as curtailing the recruitment of extremist militants and how to better communicate the uncertainty surrounding topics including climate science and intelligence forecasts.

The initial three articles in this issue remind us that public and private sector policies are often most effective when organizations identify and address the unique needs of individuals. The first investigates an important and timely question: When are immigrants vulnerable to recruitment by ideological radicals? Lyons-Padilla, Gelfand, Mirahmadi, Farooq, and Van Egmond report a fascinating survey of immigrant Muslims in the United States. These authors found that such immigrants tend to feel marginalized if they do not identify with either their culture of origin or the society in which they live. When these marginalized immigrants then experience discrimination, they tend to be more attracted to radical groups than are immigrants who have found or retained a sense of cultural identity.

Lavner, Karney, and Bradbury take on the critical question of how federal programs can most effectively promote healthy marriages among couples with low incomes. After taking stock of three large-scale field interventions, the authors suggest that a commonly used singular focus on education is unlikely to be effective. Instead, new initiatives should also address the challenging economic constraints that the couples face, which can put significant stress on relationships. Finally, Karlan, Morten, and Zinman present the findings of a study run in the Philippines—the text messaging capital of the world—that encouraged timely repayment of debts using texted reminders. Their results suggest that the personal connections in these seemingly impersonal financial transactions are of critical importance. Specifically, a personal message from a loan officer can be especially effective, but only when the borrower knows the loan officer through prior borrowing.

Three additional articles explore general-purpose policy tools that promise to extend the reach of behavioral insights to new purviews. First, Rogers, Milkman, John, and Norton address the question of how to help people translate their good intentions into positive actions such as voting or getting a flu vaccine. The authors review a body of behavioral research showing that simply prompting people to explicitly articulate a concrete and specific plan can be surprisingly effective at increasing follow-through. Second, Ho, Budescu, Dhami, and Mandel address the widely relevant issue of how expert advisers in business and government should communicate the degree of uncertainty associated with a forecast or conclusion. The authors promote a research-based approach for standardizing language used in such communications, an approach they have tested with favorable results in the climate science and intelligence analysis domains.

Castelo, Hardy, House, Mazar, Tsai, and Zhao present an example of a large-scale field experiment in which simple and virtually costless mailer design adjustments improved the effectiveness of a government service. In this case, increasing the salience of a key message on a mailer that encouraged payment of an annual automobile fee online, rather than in person, substantially increased online participation. The effect was most pronounced when messages emphasized potential gains from paying the fee on the Internet. In contrast to previous research findings in other contexts, similar messaging emphasizing losses was marginally less effective. The authors also share practical lessons they have learned from their ongoing government–academic collaboration.

Finally, in this issue, we extend the reach of *BSP* by featuring two new publication categories. In the first of our *Proposals* articles, Sah, Robertson, and Baughman take on the important topic of risks within the criminal justice system from unconscious racial bias among prosecutors. The authors argue that, whenever possible, prosecutors should be kept unaware of the race of a suspect when they are choosing whether to file a criminal charge or accept a plea deal. In fact, such blinding is not without precedent: The U.S. Department of Justice requires review committees of capital cases to examine defendant files in a race-blind manner. Second, responding to the recent surge of interest among governments, nonprofit organizations, and businesses in applying behavioral science insights, we introduce a new *Reports* category for articles that summarize and synthesize major project reports. Congdon and Shankar present the first, reviewing the projects pursued and lessons learned by the U.S. Social and Behavioral Science Team (SBST) during its first year of operation. The article also explains implications of President Obama's recent executive order directing federal agencies to work with the SBST to identify and test opportunities for applying behavioral insights to enhance the effectiveness of federal programs.

Looking forward, we are excited to report that we are receiving an increasing flow of excellent submissions to *BSP*. In coming issues, we plan to feature *Spotlight Forum* article clusters that address pressing challenges (such as enhancing the effectiveness of prekindergarten education) and emerging opportunities (such as a behavioral agenda for federal policy interventions that might be facilitated by the SBST). We welcome reader suggestions on what other topics merit emphasis on the pages of *BSP*, and we invite you to explore our new *Policyshop* blog (https://behavioralpolicy.org/blog/) to stay informed about developments in the behavioral policy world. Consider joining the Behavioral Science & Policy Association, the nonprofit community of behavioral scientists, policymakers, and other practitioners that co-publishes *BSP* with the Brookings Institution (https://behavioralpolicy.org/).

Our primary plan for this journal is to continue to feature innovative public and private sector policy solutions that draw on rigorous study of individual, group, and organizational behaviors. We look forward to continuing to extend our reach to a growing and more diverse and more international readership. As always, we welcome your feedback.

Craig R. Fox & Sim B. Sitkin
Founding Co-Editors

Belonging nowhere: Marginalization & radicalization risk among Muslim immigrants

Sarah Lyons-Padilla, Michele J. Gelfand, Hedieh Mirahmadi, Mehreen Farooq, & Marieke van Egmond

Summary.   In the last 15 years, the threat of Muslim violent extremists emerging within Western countries has grown. Terrorist organizations based in the Middle East are recruiting Muslims in the United States and Europe via social media. Yet we know little about the factors that would drive Muslim immigrants in a Western country to heed this call and become radicalized, even at the cost of their own lives. Research into the psychology of terrorism suggests that a person's cultural identity plays a key role in radicalization, so we surveyed 198 Muslims in the United States about their cultural identities and attitudes toward extremism. We found that immigrants who identify with neither their heritage culture nor the culture they are living in feel marginalized and insignificant. Experiences of discrimination make the situation worse and lead to greater support for radicalism, which promises a sense of meaning and life purpose. Such insights could be of use to policymakers engaged in efforts against violent extremism, including terrorism.

There is a critical need for academics and policy-makers to better understand the puzzle of how and why some people turn to violent extremism. Violent extremism is not limited to actions within any single faith community. It is a broad term that applies to threats emanating from a range of organizations and movements that use violence to pursue ideological, social or political goals. White supremacist movements, anarchist militias, eco-terrorists, and Muslim militants associated with terrorist organizations such as Islamic State of Iraq (ISIS) and al-Qaeda all fall in this category.

In response to violent transnational groups' increased recruitment of Muslim immigrants in Western countries, we researched factors that could contribute to the risk of radicalization among such immigrants, a potentially vulnerable demographic. Recent events make clear that this issue is becoming increasingly important both within and outside of the United States. It is estimated that more than 5,000 recruits from Europe and the United States have gone to Syria and

Lyons-Padilla, S., Gelfand, M. J., Mirahmadi, H., Farooq, M., & van Egmond, M. (2015). Belonging nowhere: Marginalization & radicalization risk among Muslim immigrants. *Behavioral Science & Policy, 1*(2).

Iraq to fight for groups such as ISIS, and some return to their countries radicalized and equipped to carry out attacks on or near their own soil.[1-3] Among these, apparently, was Belgian-born Abdelhamid Abaaoud, who led the November 2015 terrorist attacks in Paris that killed 130 people and wounded more than 350. Only a few weeks later, Syed Farook and Tashfeen Malik, an American-born citizen and a Saudi Arabian immigrant, pledged allegiance to ISIS and killed 14 people at a holiday party in San Bernardino, California. Governments around the globe need a better understanding of the root causes of such radicalization to implement successful policies to counter violent extremism (CVE), including terrorism.

While it may surprise some, evidence is strong that religion is not the primary motivator for joining violent extremists like ISIS.[4,5] In fact, research on the characteristics of violent extremists suggests that many are religious novices or converts.[6] For example, two young British men jailed in 2014 on terrorism charges had ordered *Islam for Dummies* and *The Koran for Dummies* before going to fight in Syria. Instead, religion is sometimes used to legitimize personal and collective frustrations and justify violent ideologies.

In light of the recent increase in foreign fighters for the ISIS, many of whom are first- or second-generation immigrants, more attention should be directed to immigrants' identity processes, or, in other words, how people manage their identities with their culture of origin (for example, home country or religion) and their identities with their new home country's culture. Recruiters explicitly target first- and second-generation Muslims in typically non-Muslim countries as part of their call to "embark on jihad in your own countries."[7] The vast majority of Muslim immigrants, of course, ignore the call. How can policymakers understand what draws the few immigrants who respond?

Research to date indicates that, in general, terrorists are not unusual in terms of their psychopathology or personality.[8,9] But recent studies have shown that some people who join violent extremist movements are on a quest for significance, a sense that their lives have purpose and meaning.[10,11] They want to generate this sense of worth in themselves and appear worthy in the eyes of others.[12] Personal trauma, shame, humiliation, and perceived maltreatment by society can cause people to feel a loss of self-worth, which we call *significance loss*. Individuals who have experienced such

losses of significance may be attracted to opportunities to restore a sense of self-worth and clear identity.[13-17]

Recruitment material made by Qaeda and affiliates, for example, often invoke the humiliation and suffering of Muslims throughout the world, which can resonate with people who relate to a collective experience of significance loss (see reference 12). In many propaganda videos and other recruitment efforts, committing to a violent extremist organization's definition of *jihad* is presented as a route to regaining significance. Terrorist organizations, in other words, offer a sense of belonging, purpose, and the promise of recognition and status to anyone who works on their behalf.[18] This is not unlike the sense of community that street gangs promise to American youth who lack belongingness and direction in their lives.[19]

In this context, vital questions arise for policymakers aiming to prevent violent extremism. Among the most important of these questions is which populations are at greatest risk of the loss of identity, purpose, and value? Social psychology studies offer some important clues. Michael Hogg and colleagues, for instance, have observed that joining a group with a clear ideology and strong norms reduces uncertainty among group members. The distinction between "us" versus "them" that group identification provides helps people understand who they are, what they should believe, and what to expect of others outside of their group (see references 13 and 17). For example, in one study, students from Australia who were made to feel uncertain were more likely to support an extreme group on campus and demonstrate support for its radical behavior (see reference 16). Religious groups are particularly effective at offering a sense of certainty, which may explain the appeal of violent extremist organizations for some Muslim immigrants.[20]

Building on research about immigrant acculturation, we theorized that certain Muslim immigrants and minorities who feel culturally homeless and are, in effect, marginalized lack a clear sense of belonging.[21] They, in turn, may be attracted to a supportive group that affirms their sense of self-worth and offers a clear sense of identity. We propose that marginalized immigrants are at much higher risk for feeling a loss of significance and hence are more susceptible to radicalization.

We examined this proposal with a cross-sectional survey of Muslims in the United States. To our knowledge, this is one of the first empirical studies to investigate whether and how marginalized immigrants are at risk for becoming radicalized. Our results suggest that helping Muslims become more integrated into and accepted by society and supporting their efforts to preserve aspects of their own culture could be steps that help prevent such radicalization.

Building on Existing Insights about Marginalized Immigrants

Decades ago, John Berry and colleagues[22–25] identified four different acculturation orientations that fall on two dimensions: the extent to which one maintains contact with one's heritage culture and the extent to which one forges connections with others in the larger society. These orientations apply to first-generation immigrants as well as to subsequent generations who grow up exposed to the heritage culture and the culture of the larger society. In Berry's formulation, those who primarily consider themselves part of the larger society but are not part of their own heritage culture are considered *assimilated;* those who primarily identify with their heritage culture but do not identify with the host culture are considered *separated.* Those who identify with both societies equally are *integrated,* and those who do not identify with either culture are *marginalized.* Overall, the integrated are the best off in terms of mental and physical health, success at school and work, and life satisfaction (see reference 23), and the separated and assimilated are better or worse depending on the context.[26] The marginalized do not fit in anywhere. These individuals were shown to be at risk for a number of negative outcomes in domains ranging from health to happiness to school and work adjustment (see references 22, 23, and 25).[27]

Michael Taarnby[28] and John Berry[29] have theorized that marginalization, alienation, and discrimination could be possible precursors to radicalization, although this has yet to be examined empirically. Several studies have found, though, that identity processes are important for radicalization. For example, a 2013 study of Muslim youth in the Netherlands found that feeling disconnected from Dutch society at large was an important determinant of developing a radical belief system.[30] Other research has recognized identity conflict as a risk factor for radicalization. Bernd Simon and colleagues found that Turks and Russians living in Germany showed greater sympathy for radical action when their German

and heritage culture identities were perceived to be in conflict with each other.[31] This finding highlights the importance of understanding the interplay between cultural identities and the consequences of fitting in nowhere.

In this research, we build on previous work to address a new question, namely, whether and how *marginalization*—a condition wherein individuals do not identify with either the home or the host culture and are, in effect, culturally homeless—can increase attraction to and support for extremist groups and causes among immigrants. We expect that the marginalized person experiences feelings of significance loss and may be looking for opportunities to affirm a sense of identity and self-worth (see reference 10). Building on Michael Hogg's research (see references 13–17), we propose that marginalized immigrants feel a loss of significance and can be attracted to fundamentalist groups that offer a clear sense of inclusion and purpose and the opportunity to restore a sense of self-worth.

We are also interested in the factors that strengthen the relationship between marginalization and significance loss so we can identify potential interventions for policymakers. Research on terrorism highlights the role of acute negative events—such as job loss, financial struggles, and victimization or humiliation—in radicalization processes (see reference 10).[32–35] We further propose that discrimination is one such experience that can contribute to additional significance loss among marginalized Muslim immigrants. Discrimination against Muslims has increased in the post-9/11 era, as many are subjected to name-calling, racial profiling, and negative representations of Islam in the media.[36] A study of Muslims in the Netherlands revealed that perceiving discrimination from the Dutch majority strengthened identification with the immigrant culture and weakened commitment to Dutch society.[37] Although any immigrant can be a victim of discrimination, we expect that marginalized immigrants, who already lack the sense of self-worth that is afforded by social connectedness, may be particularly jarred by outside reminders that they do not fit into society. Therefore, we predicted that the link between marginalization and significance loss is exacerbated by experiences of discrimination, which increase the appeal of fundamentalist groups and causes. Although we made no specific predictions with respect to integration, assimilation, and separation, we controlled for these factors in our analysis to look at the unique effect of marginalization on radicalization. We also examined whether they emerged as factors of risk or protection under conditions of discrimination.

We proposed a model in which marginalization relates to feelings of significance loss and those feelings, in turn, are associated with increased support for the behavior and ideologies of fundamentalist groups. We expected that experiences of discrimination would exacerbate the relationship between marginalization and a sense of significance loss. We examined this hypothesis using data from a one-time survey of nearly 200 Muslim Americans. Our findings support the proposed model, but the design of our study limits how much we can say about the dynamic, additive changes our model proposes.

A Survey of Muslim American Attitudes and Beliefs

We collaborated with an educational and community-based organization, the World Organization for Resource Development and Education (WORDE), to administer surveys among first- and second-generation Muslim immigrants in the United States. To develop our survey materials and gain a more thorough understanding of the challenges Muslims experience in American society, we conducted 20 exploratory interviews.

Potential participants were contacted through WORDE, and the survey was administered online. The survey took between 30 and 40 minutes to complete for most participants, who received a $25 Amazon.com gift card as compensation. Given the sensitive nature of this survey, drawing responses from a random sample of unsolicited respondents would have been difficult. WORDE solicited participants from its contacts database and its social media networks, which include over 3,000 individuals from diverse cultural, ethnic, and religious backgrounds. Their contact list comes from more than two decades of community building, research, and advocacy conducted by WORDE specialists across the United States. They have cultivated these relationships through programming and research initiatives in the Washington, DC, metropolitan area; Chicago; Houston; Los Angeles; Michigan; New Jersey; and New York, among other regions. Our survey focused on young adults because of the radicalization research that identifies 18- to 35-year-olds as representing the age range at the greatest risk (see reference 35).

Participants were 260 Muslims from 27 different states, but Maryland (60 participants), Virginia (35 participants), and California (30 participants) were the most strongly represented. Participants who did not meet eligibility criteria (for example, Muslim converts without a recent migrant background) or who failed to pay attention to the survey instructions were removed prior to analyses. We monitored for ineligible responses throughout the data collection process and closed the survey when we believed the number of analyzable data points met our initial sample target of 200 participants. Participants were removed from analyses if they failed more than one attention-check question, completed the survey in an unusually short time (that is, in less than 15 minutes), left large sections of the survey blank, or attempted to complete the survey more than once. We were ultimately left with 198 participants (78 male, 107 female, 13 who did not report gender; mean age = 27.42 years). In this sample, 92 were first-generation immigrants and 105 were second-generation Americans. We sampled from more than 20 heritage country backgrounds, but more than half (105 participants) identified Pakistan as their heritage country.

Because of the sensitive nature of the survey content, we took several steps to ensure anonymity and confidentiality. Before providing consent to take part in the survey, participants first read a description of the purpose of the research, which was to understand more about the experiences of Muslims in the United States. We emphasized that identifying information would not be collected and encouraged participants to answer as honestly as possible, mentioning that some questions might be difficult to answer. The survey first asked participants about their cultural identity and experiences of discrimination in the United States. Then participants answered questions about their general psychological state, including items measuring a sense of significance loss. Questions about radicalization were placed near the end of the survey. Finally, participants completed a section of demographic questions. (A detailed description of our research methods is available online in the Supplemental Material.)

Querying about Risk Factors

Our survey used questionnaires with scaled responses to ask about marginalization, assimilation, separation, integration, experiences of discrimination, and feelings of significance loss. We measured support for radicalism in two ways. We included questions that assessed support for a radical interpretation of Islam and presented participants with a description of a hypothetical group modeled after the attributes of violent extremist organizations. Participants were asked to indicate how much they thought people in their social circle would support such a group.

Acculturation

The measure of acculturation tapped into respondents' own feelings about their cultural customs and values, specifically with respect to integration ("I wish to maintain my heritage culture values and also adopt key features of American values"), assimilation ("I wish to give up my heritage culture values for the sake of adopting American values"), separation ("I wish to maintain my heritage culture customs rather than adopt American customs"), and marginalization ("I do not wish to maintain my heritage culture values or adopt American values as I feel uncomfortable with both types of values").

Our preliminary interviews suggested that one's identity as a Muslim is just as important as one's identity from one's country of origin, so we supplemented our measure of marginalization with two questions about Muslim culture rather than the heritage country: "There are times when I feel like I don't belong to any culture" and "Sometimes I don't feel part of American culture or part of Muslim culture."

Discrimination

We included an eight-item scale based on previous work on discrimination against Muslims.[38] Sample items include "Have you ever experienced hostility or unfair treatment because of your religion?" and "Have you ever experienced hostility or unfair treatment because of your cultural background?" Items were measured on a five-point scale ranging from 1 = *never* to 5 = *all of the time.*

Significance Loss

We adapted the 24-item Need Threat Scale[39–41] with subscales for belongingness, meaningful existence, control, and self-esteem, as these are all needs thought to be captured in the quest for significance. We added four of our own items pertaining to humiliation, shame,

hopelessness, and anger. These items were derived from interview responses as well as previous work on significance loss (see reference 10). Participants were asked to indicate on a five-point scale how often they felt different states and emotions.

Support for a Radical Interpretation of Islam

We included 10 items representing a radical interpretation of certain tenets of Islam, such as the meaning of jihad.[42] Sample items include "Muslims in America should help their oppressed brothers and sisters in other parts of the world by participating in combative jihad"; "It is important to give to Islamic charities, even if their ideological beliefs may be extreme at times"; and "Combative jihad is the only way to conduct jihad."

Support for Fundamentalist Groups

We presented participants with a description of a hypothetical fundamentalist group made up of young Muslims in the United States. The text was modeled after other radicalization research and adapted to fit the religious context (see reference 16). The description was tested in advance to ensure that the group was perceived as neither too extreme nor too mainstream. The hypothetical group made clear their stance against American maltreatment of Muslims and promised belongingness, commitment, and loyalty to potential members. Although violence was never explicitly mentioned, the hypothetical group justified extreme actions to support its cause. The full text can be obtained by contacting the authors.

Drawing from the the literature on the psychology of radicalization (see reference 16 and reference 31), we asked participants how much they thought most people they know would like the hypothetical group, how willing these friends would be to engage in activities on behalf of the group, and to what extent their friends would sympathize with the group should it engage in extreme behaviors. Because we expected that many participants would be reluctant to express their true opinions if they were asked about their own attraction to the group, rather than ask for their own opinions, we asked participants to indicate the extent to which most people they knew would be interested in the group, a framing approach that has been used in other research as a substitute for measuring individual attitudes.[43,44] We formed a 12-item composite measure from these questions.

Measuring Potential Factors Contributing to Radicalization

We used a statistical method called *moderated mediation analysis*[45] to test our hypothesis that feelings of marginalization and significance loss would predict support for fundamentalist groups and causes. This allowed us to look at whether and how intermediary processes such as discrimination might explain the relationship between the two variables. We also wanted to examine how these relationships might change in response to additional experiences such as integration, assimilation, and separation. We ran the analyses twice to see connections with support for radical beliefs and support for fundamentalist groups. (A detailed description of our results is included in the online Supplemental Material. Supplemental Figures 1 and 2, for example, depict the moderated mediation relationship for each indicator of support for radicalism, and the unstandardized loadings with standard errors are provided in the text.)

Support for a Radical Interpretation of Islam

As expected, feelings of marginalization predicted a greater sense of significance loss. So did experiences of discrimination. Moreover, the relationship between marginalization and significance loss became stronger with more experiences of discrimination. In this formulation, feeling a loss of significance predicted support for radical interpretations of Islam.

Support for Fundamentalist Groups

As before, marginalization and discrimination were found to predict feelings of significance loss. This relationship between marginalization and significance loss became stronger with the experience of more discrimination. In turn, significance loss predicted attraction to fundamentalist groups. This analysis is in line with our prediction that marginalization could be related to attraction to fundamentalist groups if a person feels a loss of significance and high degrees of discrimination.

Although we focused primarily on the role of marginalization in this study, we also looked at the implications of other acculturation factors. Strong feelings of integration ran counter to a loss of significance. Assimilation, though, was unrelated to any of the variables of interest. Feelings of separation were associated with an increased risk for supporting radical interpretations of Islam. Marginalization was the only factor of acculturation that related to increased significance loss (see Figures 1 and 2).

We tested interactions between the other acculturation variables and experiences of discrimination to determine whether any of them might be factors for risk or protection. We found two notable interactions. First, the more participants felt integrated, the less discrimination was associated with significance loss. Second, although separation by itself did not predict significance loss, it apparently did when it was paired with higher levels of discrimination.

Relevance to Extremist Group Recruitment

Terror attacks committed from within by a target country's citizens and by established immigrants have risen steadily in the past few years.[46] For instance, the 2013 Boston Marathon bombing was committed by brothers Tamerlan and Dzhokhar Tsarnaev, ethnic Chechen Muslims who had been in the United States for more than 10 years. The younger brother, Dzhokhar, was a naturalized U.S. citizen enrolled in an American college. Faisal Shahzad, who was foiled in an attempt to detonate a car bomb in Times Square in 2010, was also a naturalized American citizen. The two horrifying terror attacks on Paris in 2015 were led by Muslim men born in France and Belgium. Similarly, the late 2015 shooting rampage in San Bernardino, California, was led by a husband and wife; one was born in Chicago, the other was an immigrant born in Pakistan. Policymakers clearly need to be able to identify risk factors for the radicalization of established immigrants and to understand the psychological processes that attract at-risk individuals to violent extremist groups, with an eye toward creating effective prevention-oriented interventions.

Some counterterrorism experts have postulated a link between radicalization and identity struggles (see reference 2),[47] and our research provides some of the first data supporting this relationship. Our results showed that marginalized immigrants in the United States may be at much greater risk for feeling a loss of significance, which, in turn, may be related to increased support

Figure 1. Model showing the effect of marginalization on support for a radical interpretation of Islam is not direct but occurs via significance loss. The effect of marginalization on significance loss is exacerbated by experiences of discrimination.

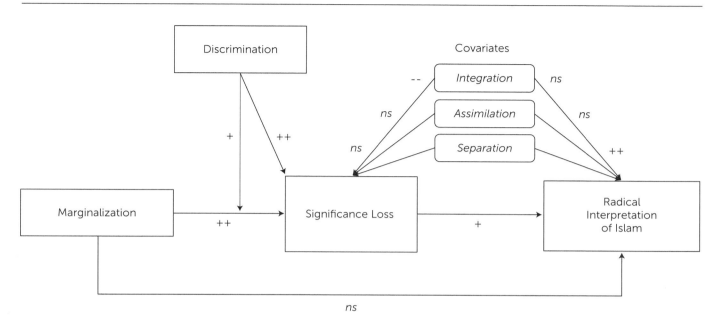

ns = the relationship between the variables was not significant; + = a significant positive relationship at the $p < .05$ level; ++ = a highly significant positive relationship at the $p < .001$ level. -- = a highly significant negative relationship.

Figure 2. Model showing the effect of marginalization on support for the fundamentalist group is not direct but occurs via significance loss. The effect of marginalization on significance loss is exacerbated by experiences of discrimination.

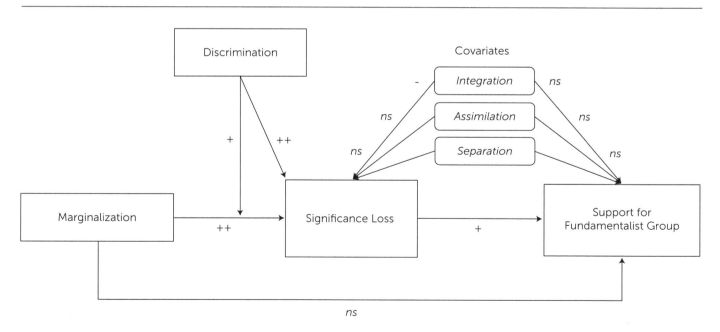

ns = the relationship between the variables was not significant; + = a significant positive relationship at the $p < .05$ level; - = a significant negative relationship; ++ = a highly significant positive relationship at the $p < .001$ level.

for fundamentalist groups and ideologies. A loss of significance stemming from personal trauma, shame, humiliation, and perceived maltreatment is associated with increased support for radicalism. Experiences of discrimination exacerbate this process. Discrimination by others in the larger society was associated with amplified feelings of a loss of significance, which, in turn, predicted support for fundamentalist groups and causes. Marginalization and discrimination are particularly potent when experienced in tandem.

Feelings of marginalization were the only acculturation variable associated with significance loss, because all of the other factors of acculturation could provide some sense of social identity and self-worth. Immigrants who were more integrated did not experience as much loss of significance as a result of discrimination, compared with their less integrated peers. However, our data suggest individuals who feel strongly tied to their heritage culture may suffer from significance loss when they feel discriminated against. Because we found that a loss of significance is associated with increased support for radicalism, it should raise concern that not only is discrimination related to an overall threatened sense of self-worth but that such experiences are particularly damaging for marginalized and separated immigrants.

This study cannot prove definitively what causes the radicalization of immigrants. The design of our study limits our ability to fully test our process-based model of immigrant radicalization. We might know more about that process if we had been able to administer the survey a second time, but that would have required collecting identifying information about our subjects so that we could follow up. Given our concern about participants answering sensitive questions honestly, we decided not to ask participants for their contact information.

We measured correlations, not causes. Although we feel our model offers a persuasive explanation, one also might propose that the causal arrows in the model run in the opposite direction. For example, it could be that support for radicalization leads to a loss of significance, which, in turn, causes immigrants to feel marginalized and excluded. It is also plausible that individuals who develop radical belief systems become distanced from moderate Muslims and the larger society. It is also possible that a loss of significance could add to a sense of withdrawal and increased perceptions of exclusion. Given the significance-restoring properties of extreme

groups, however, we think it is unlikely that support for radicalism would cause significance loss (see references 10 and 18).

Our study does not allow us to assess feedback loops that might propel the variables in the model. For example, it is possible that these processes form an additive loop in which marginalized individuals who experience discrimination become attracted to fundamentalist groups and, through their involvement in such groups, begin to feel further marginalized. Likewise, individuals who feel separate from society and who have developed radical ideologies may strengthen their identification with their heritage group, ultimately becoming more separated from the broader society. In the future, researchers could use longitudinal designs that measure individuals' experiences, feelings, and ideologies at multiple points in time to capture the dynamic process of immigrant marginalization and radicalization.

Because this study was based on a self-report survey, it could not measure actual radical thought and action. Some participants may not have answered the radicalism questions completely honestly because of social strictures or concern about being identified. We attempted to address this problem by recruiting participants through a trusted organization, by emphasizing that responses were totally anonymous, and by including radicalism measures that were not framed too directly (that is, we asked participants how much people in their social circle would support the hypothetical fundamentalist group). In the future, researchers should attempt to replicate these results in a randomized sample that is more broadly representative of American Muslims than was possible with our sample.

For practical reasons, it was impossible for us to measure actual extremism. Our results should not be taken to mean that individuals who are marginalized or excluded and experience significance loss will eventually join a violent extremism movement, but they may be at increased risk to do so. Presumably many individuals bear grievances against their host societies without ever engaging in violence.

Insights of Use to Policymakers

Recognizing the threat that violent extremism poses for national security, some political figures have taken a "better safe than sorry" approach, proposing limits on the acceptance of Syrian refugees and other Muslim migrants as well as programs to monitor Muslims already on American soil. However, our data suggest that anti-Muslim rhetoric is likely to be counterproductive. Exclusionary policies reinforce the ISIS narrative that the West is anti-Islam, increasing its appeal for Muslims who are feeling marginalized and discriminated against and looking for opportunities to regain significance. We should not confuse being anti-ISIS with being anti-Islam.

We surmise that many of the counterterrorism initiatives and surveillance policies currently being used to identify violent extremists may actually paradoxically fuel support for extremism. Recent examples of homegrown plots lend support to this notion. For example, the failed Times Square bomber, Faisal Shahzad, felt angry about the treatment of Muslims in the United States and the West more generally following the September 11 attacks, as well as about American military intervention in Iraq under the pretense of searching for weapons of mass destruction. He told authorities that he had struggled to find a peaceful but effective way to cope before ultimately attempting to set off a car bomb in 2010.[48] Racial profiling and spying programs in the post-9/11 era that target Muslims are likely to induce feelings of perceived discrimination or exclusion and contribute to a sense of significance loss. Our findings should help to discourage policymakers from designing programs that aggravate or perpetuate hostility between the immigrant Muslim community and the Western governments under which they live.

The reality is that more than three million Muslims are already living in the United States[49] and more than thirteen million are living in Western Europe.[50] Efforts to prevent radicalization within Muslim communities are more likely to succeed if they focus on achieving integration rather than alienation. To this end, our data suggest several strategies. First, Muslims in the United States should not be forced to choose between American and Muslim identities. This means helping the moderate Muslim majority become more integrated into and accepted by society without being pressured to give up important aspects of their own culture, including but not limited to language, religious articles of clothing, dietary customs, and observance of religious rituals and holidays. Significance loss could be forestalled if American Muslims are able to develop an American identity without having to give up their cultural heritage. Integration strategies that provide opportunities for Muslim immigrants to actively maintain their multiple cultural identities may be able to reduce their vulnerability to marginalization and radicalization.

Unfortunately, fostering a more welcoming climate for integration is not as simple as hosting an ad campaign to promote a more positive image of Islam in society or stifling discriminatory discourse. Policymakers and society at large must acknowledge that a multicultural country's identity is derived from diverse sources of cultural influence, including meaningful contributions from individuals with a Muslim heritage.

Young Muslims who are at risk and feeling marginalized and discriminated against may be guided toward nonviolent groups that have significance-restoring effects on participants. Future researchers should search for groups and activities that provide attractive alternatives to violent extremist organizations that satisfy needs for significance.

In the United States, the federal government has proposed educational and cultural exchange projects geared toward promoting diversity, tolerance, and minority integration. The White House is looking to build community resilience programs for at-risk youth through technical skills training and opportunities for civic education, community service, and empowerment. Our research suggests that these types of programs hold promise, particularly if they focus on the acceptance of multiple identities and provide psychological inoculation against feeling a loss of significance. Obviously such government programs should be measured and evaluated to see whether they are successful in providing alternative avenues for at-risk youth to feel gains in significance and self-worth.

There are some real-world examples of how providing alternative avenues toward feeling significant can derail support for radicalism. One deradicalization program in Sri Lanka offered detained members of the Tamil Tigers vocational education programs that increased their sense of self-efficacy and prepared them for their reintegration into society. When compared with a control group, these individuals demonstrated decreased support for the violent struggle against the Sinhalese over time (see reference 11).[51] In the city of Aarhus, Denmark, law enforcement partnered with the Muslim community to approach at-risk individuals and steer them away from engaging in violent extremism. The program has experienced some success and may reduce the likelihood of immigrants becoming marginalized and excluded.[52]

Our data only included a sample from the United States, but as recent events painfully demonstrate, homegrown radicalization and immigrant marginalization are not uniquely American problems. In the wake of the 2015 Paris attacks, Muslims in France have been telling global media that they struggle to be accepted as part of French society and feel restricted in expressing their Muslim identities in public spaces.[53] Fear-based discriminatory responses, such as France's 2010 ban on face-covering burqas and hijabs, merely reinforce anti-Muslim sentiment and lead to further disengagement of the Muslim community. In the United Kingdom, the Prime Minister's Task Force on Tackling Radicalisation and Extremism developed a counter-radicalization strategy to intervene at sites thought to be hotbeds for radicalization, including universities. In practice, British students who show signs of religiosity or political activism are often viewed with suspicion because of concern that they are at risk for radicalization.[54,55]

Radicalization is now a global problem, so researchers will need to examine whether the model we studied here reflects the dynamics of radicalization in countries outside of the United States. For example, radicalization processes might be even more pronounced among individuals who feel marginalized or segregated in societies that have higher degrees of ethnocentrism and negative attitudes toward outsiders.[56] As our research advances, we are collecting data on immigrant acculturation processes and radicalization in Germany and other countries.

Violent extremism can no longer be considered a threat solely from the outside by Western nations. Groups working on counterterrorism efforts must look inward to ask what in our societies provides a fertile breeding ground for radicalism and motivates people to join extremist groups and causes, even at the cost of their own lives. Our research has shown that immigrant identity processes are an important contributing factor. We hope that attention to these findings might result in more effective homeland security policies focusing on prevention, more resources, and more accepting neighbors for Muslim communities in Western nations. This research suggests that finding ways to help at-risk individuals gain a sense of significance and belonging may be one promising strategy for preventing future acts of homegrown terrorism in some societies.

author affiliation

Lyons-Padilla and Gelfand, Department of Psychology, University of Maryland; Mirahmadi and Farooq, World Organization for Resource Development and Education; van Egmond, Bremen International Graduate School of Social Sciences, Jacobs University, Bremen. Corresponding author's e-mail: sarahlp@stanford.edu.

author note

This research was supported by the Science and Technology Directorate of the U.S. Department of Homeland Security through Study of Terrorism and Behavior Grant 2012-ST-61-CS0001 made to the National Consortium on the Study of Terrorism and Responses to Terrorism (START). The views and conclusions contained in this article are those of the authors and should not be interpreted as necessarily representing the official policies, either expressed or implied, of the U.S. Department of Homeland Security or START. This research was also funded by an Anneliese Maier Research Award from the Humboldt Foundation and Office of Naval Research Grant 019183-001 awarded to Michele Gelfand. We also thank Arie Kruglanski and the START research group at the University of Maryland for their input throughout the research process.

supplemental material ⌐↗⌐

- http://behavioralpolicy.org/vol-1-no-2/lyons
- Methods & Analysis
- Additional References

References

1. Barrett, R. (2015). *Foreign fighters: An updated assessment of the flow of foreign fighters into Syria and Iraq.* Retrieved from the Soufan Group website: http://soufangroup.com/wp-content/uploads/2015/12/TSG_ForeignFightersUpdate4.pdf
2. Benac, N., & Riechmann, D. (2014, September 20). Tracing shift from everyday American to jihadis. Associated Press. Retrieved from http://bigstory.ap.org/article/3d58257d6abc4ee384644f99503f0e83/tracing-shift-everyday-american-jihadis
3. U.S. House of Representatives, Committee on Homeland Security. (2014, September 17). FBI, DHS, NCTC heads agree: ISIS recruitment and radicalization of Americans dangerous and difficult to track [Press release]. Retrieved from http://homeland.house.gov/press-release/fbi-dhs-nctc-heads-agree-isis-recruitment-and-radicalization-americans-dangerous-and

4. Pearce, E. (2014, September 3). ISIS and the politics of radicalization [Blog post]. Retrieved from http://www.brookings.edu/blogs/iran-at-saban/posts/2014/09/03-pearce-isis-and-the-politics-of-radicalization

5. Butler, D. (2015, December 3). Terrorism science: 5 insights into jihad in Europe. *Nature, 528*, 20–21. doi:10.1038/528020a

6. Roy, O. (2015, November). *What is the driving force behind jihadist terrorism? A scientific perspective on the causes/circumstances of joining the scene* [Speech]. Available from Bundeskriminalamt Autumn Conference website: http://www.bka.de/nn_195186/EN/Publications/AutumnConferences/2015/autumnConferences2015__node.html?__nnn=true

7. Rosenbach, M., & Stark, H. (2011, May 11). German jihad: Homegrown terror takes on new dimensions. *Spiegel Online International*. Retrieved from http://www.spiegel.de/international/germany/german-jihad-homegrown-terror-takes-on-new-dimensions-a-761391.html

8. Atran, S. (2003, March 7). Genesis of suicide terrorism. *Science, 299*, 1534–1539. doi:10.1126/science.1078854

9. Horgan, J. (2003). The search for the terrorist personality. In A. Silke (Ed.), *Terrorists, victims and society: Psychological perspectives on terrorism and its consequences* (pp. 3–27). Chichester, United Kingdom: Wiley.

10. Kruglanski, A. W., Chen, X., Dechesne, M., Fishman, S., & Orehek, E. (2009). Fully committed: Suicide bombers' motivation and the quest for personal significance. *Political Psychology, 30*, 331–357. doi:10.1111/j.1467-9221.2009.00698.x

11. Kruglanski, A. W., Gelfand, M. J., Bélanger, J. J., Sheveland, A., Hettiarachchi, M., & Gunaratna, R. (2014). The psychology of radicalization and deradicalization: How significance quest impacts violent extremism. *Political Psychology, 35*, 69–93. doi:10.1111/pops.12163

12. Kruglanski, A. W., Bélanger, J. J., Gelfand, M., Gunaratna, R., Hettiarachchi, M., Reinares, F., . . . Sharvit, K. (2013). Terrorism—A (self) love story: Redirecting the significance quest can end violence. *American Psychologist, 68*, 559–575. doi:10.1037/a0032615

13. Hogg, M. A. (2012). Uncertainty-identity theory. In P. A. M. Van Lange, A. W. Kruglanski, & E. T. Higgins (Eds.), *Handbook of theories of social psychology* (Vol. 2, pp. 62–80). Thousand Oaks, CA: Sage.

14. Hogg, M. A. (2014). From uncertainty to extremism: Social categorization and identity processes. *Current Directions in Psychological Science, 23*, 338–342.

15. Hogg, M. A., & Adelman, J. (2013). Uncertainty–identity theory: Extreme groups, radical behavior, and authoritarian leadership. *Journal of Social Issues, 69*, 436–454.

16. Hogg, M. A., Meehan, C., & Farquharson, J. (2010). The solace of radicalism: Self-uncertainty and group identification in the face of threat. *Journal of Experimental Social Psychology, 46*, 1061–1066. doi:10.1016/j.jesp.2010.05.005

17. Hogg, M. A., Sherman, D. K., Dierselhuis, J., Maitner, A. T., & Moffitt, G. (2007). Uncertainty, entitativity, and group identification. *Journal of Experimental Social Psychology, 43*, 135–142. doi:10.1016/j.jesp.2005.12.008

18. Crenshaw, M. (2007). Explaining suicide terrorism: A review essay. *Security Studies, 16*, 133–162.

19. McMillan, D. W., & Chavis, D. M. (1986). Sense of community: A definition and theory. *Journal of Community Psychology, 14*, 6–23.

20. Hogg, M. A., Adelman, J. R., & Blagg, R. D. (2010). Religion in the face of uncertainty: An uncertainty-identity theory account of religiousness. *Personality and Social Psychology Review, 14*, 72–83.

21. Stroink, M. L. (2007). Processes and preconditions underlying terrorism in second-generation immigrants. *Peace and Conflict: Journal of Peace Psychology, 13*, 293–312. doi:10.1080/10781910701471322

22. Berry, J. W. (1970). Marginality, stress and ethnic identification in an acculturated aboriginal community. *Journal of Cross-Cultural Psychology, 1*, 239–252. doi:10.1177/135910457000100303

23. Berry, J. W. (1997). Immigration, acculturation, and adaptation. *Applied Psychology: An International Review, 46*, 5–34. doi:10.1080/026999497378467

24. Berry, J. W. (2003). Conceptual approaches to acculturation. In K. M. Chun, P. B. Organista, & G. Marín (Eds.), *Acculturation: Advances in theory, measurement, and applied research* (pp. 17–37). Washington, DC: American Psychological Association.

25. Sam, D. L., & Berry, J. W. (2010). Acculturation: When individuals and groups of different cultural backgrounds meet. *Perspectives on Psychological Science, 5*, 472–481. doi:10.1177/1745691610373075

26. Cohen, S., & Wills, T. A. (1985). Stress, social support, and the buffering hypothesis. *Psychological Bulletin, 98*, 310–357. doi:10.1037/0033-2909.98.2.310

27. Berry, J. W. (2006). Contexts of acculturation. In D. L. Sam & J. W. Berry (Eds.), *The Cambridge handbook of acculturation psychology* (pp. 27–42). New York, NY: Cambridge University Press.

28. Taarnby, M. (2005). *Recruitment of Islamist terrorists in Europe: Trends and perspectives* [Research report]. Retrieved from Investigative Project on Terrorism website: http://www.investigativeproject.org/documents/testimony/58.pdf

29. Berry, J. W. (2007, June). *Are immigrant youth at risk for radicalization?* Paper presented at the 68th Annual Canadian Psychological Association Conference, Ottawa, Ontario, Canada.

30. Doosje, B., Loseman, A., & van den Bos, K. (2013). Determinants of radicalization of Islamic youth in the Netherlands: Personal uncertainty, perceived injustice, and perceived group threat. *Journal of Social Issues, 69*, 586–604.

31. Simon, B., Reichert, F., & Grabow, O. (2013). When dual identity becomes a liability: Identity and political radicalism among migrants. *Psychological Science, 24*, 251–257. doi:10.1177/0956797612450889

32. King, M., & Taylor, D. M. (2011). The radicalization of homegrown jihadists: A review of theoretical models and social psychological evidence. *Terrorism and Political Violence, 23*, 602–622. doi:10.1080/09546553.2011.587064

33. Moghaddam, F. M. (2005). The staircase to terrorism: A psychological exploration. *American Psychologist, 60*, 161–169. doi:10.1037/0003-066X.60.2.161

34. Sageman, M. (2004). *Understanding terror networks*. Philadelphia: University of Pennsylvania Press.

35. Silber, M. D., & Bhatt, A. (2007). *Radicalization in the West: The homegrown threat*. New York, NY: New York City Police Department.

36. Sirin, S. R., & Fine, M. (2007). Hyphenated selves: Muslim American youth negotiating identities on the fault lines of global conflict. *Applied Developmental Science, 11*, 151–163. doi:10.1080/10888690701454658

37. Verkuyten, M., & Yildiz, A. A. (2007). National (dis)identification and ethnic and religious identity: A study among Turkish–Dutch Muslims. *Personality and Social Psychology Bulletin, 33*, 1448–1462. doi:10.1177/0146167207304276

38. Fleischmann, F., Phalet, K., & Klein, O. (2011). Religious identification and politicization in the face of discrimination:

Support for political Islam and political action among the Turkish and Moroccan second generation in Europe. *British Journal of Social Psychology, 50,* 628–648. doi:10.1111/j.2044-8309.2011.02072.x

39. Jamieson, J. P., Harkins, S. G., & Williams, K. D. (2010). Need threat can motivate performance after ostracism. *Personality and Social Psychology Bulletin, 36,* 690–702. doi:10.1177/0146167209358882

40. Williams, K. D. (2009). Ostracism: A temporal need-threat model. In M. P. Zanna (Ed.), *Advances in experimental social psychology* (Vol. 41, pp. 275–314). London, United Kingdom: Elsevier.

41. Zadro, L., Williams, K. D., & Richardson, R. (2004). How low can you go? Ostracism by a computer is sufficient to lower self-reported levels of belonging, control, self-esteem, and meaningful existence. *Journal of Experimental Social Psychology, 40,* 560–567.

42. Kruglanski, A. W., Gelfand, M. J., Sheveland, A., Babush, M., Hetiarachchi, M., Bonto, M. N., & Gunaratna, R. (2015). *What a difference two years make: Patterns of radicalization in a Philippine jail.* Unpublished manuscript.

43. Chiu, C.-Y., Gelfand, M. J., Yamagishi, T., Shteynberg, G., & Wan, C. (2010). Intersubjective culture: The role of intersubjective perceptions in cross-cultural research. *Perspectives on Psychological Science, 5,* 482–493.

44. Shteynberg, G., Gelfand, M. J., & Kim, K. (2009). Peering into the "Magnum Mysterium" of culture: The explanatory power of descriptive norms. *Journal of Cross-Cultural Psychology, 40,* 46–69.

45. Hayes, A. F. (2012). *PROCESS: A versatile computational tool for observed variable mediation, moderation, and conditional process modeling* [White paper]. Retrieved from http://www.afhayes.com/public/process2012.pdf

46. Bjelopera, J. P., & Randol, M. A. (2010). *American jihadist terrorism: Combating a complex threat.* Washington, DC: Congressional Research Service.

47. Trianni, F., & Katz, A. (2014, September 5). Why Westerners are fighting for ISIS. *TIME.* Retrieved from http://time.com/3270896/isis-iraq-syria-western-fighters/

48. Elliott, A., Tavernise, S., & Barnard, A. (2010, May 15). For Times Sq. suspect, long roots of discontent. *New York Times.* Retrieved from http://www.nytimes.com/2010/05/16/nyregion/16suspect.html

49. Mohamed, B. (2016, January 6). A new estimate of the U.S. Muslim population. Retrieved from Pew Research Center website: http://www.pewresearch.org/fact-tank/2016/01/06/a-new-estimate-of-the-u-s-muslim-population/

50. Hackett, C. (2015, November 17). 5 facts about the Muslim population in Europe. Pew Research Center. Retrieved from Pew Research Center website: http://www.pewresearch.org/fact-tank/2015/11/17/5-facts-about-the-muslim-population-in-europe/

51. Dugas, M., & Kruglanski, A. W. (2014). The quest for significance model of radicalization: Implications for the management of terrorist detainees. *Behavioral Sciences & the Law, 32,* 423–439.

52. Crouch, D., & Henley, J. (2015, February 23). A way home for jihadis: Denmark's radical approach to Islamic extremism. *Guardian.* Retrieved from http://www.theguardian.com/world/2015/feb/23/home-jihadi-denmark-radical-islamic-extremism-aarhus-model-scandinavia

53. Andre, V., Mansouri, F., & Lobo, M. (2015). A fragmented discourse of religious leadership in France: Muslim youth between citizenship and radicalization. *Journal of Muslim Minority Affairs, 35,* 296–313.

54. Prime Minister's Task Force on Radicalisation and Extremism. (2013). *Tackling extremism in the UK: Report from the Prime Minister's Task Force on Radicalisation and Extremism.* Retrieved from Her Majesty's Government website: https://www.gov.uk/government/uploads/system/uploads/attachment_data/file/263181/ETF_FINAL.pdf

55. Brown, K. E., & Saeed, T. (2014). Radicalization and counter-radicalization at British universities: Muslim encounters and alternatives. *Ethnic and Racial Studies, 38*(11), 1–17.

56. Gelfand, M. J., Raver, J. L., Nishii, L., Leslie, L. M., Lun, J., Lim, B. C., . . . Yamaguchi, S. (2011, May 27). Differences between tight and loose cultures: A 33-nation study. *Science, 332,* 1100–1104.

New directions for policies aimed at strengthening low-income couples

Justin A. Lavner, Benjamin R. Karney, & Thomas N. Bradbury

Summary. Strong marriages are associated with a range of positive outcomes for adults and their children. But many couples struggle to build and sustain strong marriages. Federal initiatives have sought to support marriage, particularly among low-income populations, through programs that emphasize relationship education. Recent results from three large-scale interventions funded by these initiatives are weaker than expected. These results provide a valuable opportunity to ask what policy strategies would work better. Research demonstrating how economic strain affects low-income families and constrains their individual well-being, relationship satisfaction, communication, and parenting is relevant here. So is research indicating that addressing the financial pressures low-income couples face can improve relationship stability. An increased emphasis on these programs, either alone or in combination with relationship education, could better serve low-income couples.

When Janet lost her housekeeping job at the hospital, it felt like an earthquake had struck the office where she received the news. The ground under her chair felt unsteady. A roar erupted between her ears, preventing her from hearing what her supervisor said about when to give back her ID card. In the weeks that followed, Janet's panic faded, in good part because she could lean on her husband. The hours he spent listening to her shock and disappointment were an emotional salve. Just as important was her confidence that his pay could, at least for a while, cover the rent while she looked for work.

Strong, healthy marriages have been associated with a range of benefits for adults and their children. Married adults report better emotional, financial, and physical well-being than do divorced adults.[1] And adults in more satisfying marriages report better relationships with their friends and relatives, increased ability to function at work, lower levels of general distress, and better perceived health compared with adults in lower-quality marriages.[2] Children whose parents remain married do better academically, socially, and psychologically than children whose parents divorce.[3] The same is true for children whose parents have little marital conflict.[4]

Lavner, J. A., Karney, B. R., & Bradbury, T. N. (2015). New directions for policies aimed at strengthening low-income couples. *Behavioral Science & Policy, 1*(2).

Unfortunately, many couples struggle to build and sustain healthy marriages. As many as 30% of intact couples are estimated to be significantly dissatisfied with their relationships,[5] and 33% of first marriages dissolve within the first 10 years.[6] Divorce rates are especially high among couples living in low-income communities, where 69% of marriages end within the first 10 years.[7] Moreover, many couples do not get married at all—and marriage rates are especially low among couples with low socioeconomic status, such as those with a high school diploma or less.[8] The percentage of children born to unmarried parents has surged over the last several decades: In 2010, 40% of all children born in the United States had unmarried parents.[9] The relationship stability of low-income couples who are unmarried at the time of their child's birth is precarious: Within a year, 22% will end their romantic relationship and only 9% will marry.[10]

Policymakers have recently sought to combat these trends among low-income families with several large-scale federal relationship-education programs, each serving several thousand low-income couples. But evaluations of these expensive interventions reveal minimal, if any, benefits to the couples that enrolled. And because most studies in this area have focused on these large-scale interventions, no research yet clarifies what sort of program would yield better results.[11] Despite that, we have identified a different approach to assisting couples and their families that merits exploration. Studies independent of these evaluations highlight the negative impact of financial stress on these relationships. And some evaluations show that programs that reduce the financial stresses experienced by families with low incomes can improve the stability of these families. These findings suggest that promoting more economic security among low-income couples may be a promising alternative path for intervention. We will describe more about this conclusion in detail below. But first let's look closely at evaluations of the funded interventions.

Federal Efforts to Strengthen Marriage through Relationship Education

The federal government began trying to strengthen families with low incomes by promoting marriage in 1996. In that year the Personal Responsibility and Work Opportunity Reconciliation Act (a welfare reform law)

sanctioned marriage programs as an acceptable use of Temporary Assistance to Needy Families (TANF) funds. Funding increased in 2002, when President George W. Bush launched the Healthy Marriage Initiative, diverting more than $100 million from existing programs to fund demonstration projects intended to strengthen couple relationships.[12] This amount increased again in 2005, when the Deficit Reduction Act of 2005 allocated $150 million per year from 2006 to 2010 to promote healthy marriages and responsible fatherhood through a variety of programs. Funding has continued since that time; the most recent funding proposal in May 2015 was expected to allocate over $50 million in support of healthy marriage and relationship programming.[13]

All of these initiatives have made expanded access to relationship education the primary tool to improve couples' relationships and promote marriage.[14] Most relationship education programs are based on behavioral theory, which argues that couples become distressed because they have not developed or maintained key skills such as providing empathic and supportive communication and effective problem solving.[15] Because these skills are seen as the driver of relationship satisfaction, relationship education focuses on teaching couples new skills to improve the overall health of their relationship. For example, these group workshops discuss skills relating to improving communication and conflict management, building affection and intimacy, and managing the transition to parenthood. Workshops also address topics such as developing trust and commitment, maintaining fidelity, considering marriage, and working together financially.[16]

Prior to these federal initiatives focusing on couples with low incomes, relationship education had been developed and tested almost exclusively among middle-class, Caucasian couples. Research in these more affluent samples suggested that such programs offered small-to-medium benefits in relationship satisfaction and positive and negative communication three to six months posttreatment.[17] Given these positive results, the U.S. Administration of Children and Families (ACF), a division of the Department of Health and Human Services, adapted these programs for low-income populations. These types of relationship-education programs typically had not served low-income couples, and greater access was seen as potentially beneficial to them and their children. ACF funded three large-scale evaluations to test this possibility. All three evaluations took place at multiple sites and lasted for several years. One of the three was nonexperimental in design and focused on community-level changes. In the two others, couples were randomly assigned to either participate in the relationship education group or be in a control group that received no intervention.

In many ways, the evaluation results are disappointing. The interventions produced weaker-than-hoped-for outcomes among couples, despite the millions of dollars invested in the programs. That said, the evaluations offer a valuable opportunity for policymakers and researchers to ask how these programs could be made better. More specifically, what strategies would substantially assist people with low incomes in their efforts to sustain or improve relationships with their spouses or romantic partners? Guided by relevant research separate from these evaluations, we see strong merit in focusing on helping couples with a persistent source of strife: the economic insecurities many contend with. But first, let's explain what existing couple-support programs do and do not do, as well as their outcomes.

What Federal Initiatives Did and Did Not Accomplish

Community Healthy Marriage Initiative

CHMI was the largest-scale intervention supported by this initiative. This nonexperimental study examined community-wide efforts aimed at improving relationship skills and increasing the health of marriages among couples living in low-income communities. Target communities of 100,000 to 200,000 residents from three cities (Dallas, Texas; St. Louis, Missouri; and Milwaukee, Wisconsin) were included. The programs included direct services, such as relationship and marriage education classes and retreats, and indirect media and outreach services, such as advertisements and public events to attract participants and public service announcements about the importance of marriage (see reference 14). The control group consisted of matched communities from three comparison cities (Fort Worth, Texas; Kansas City, Missouri; and Cleveland, Ohio), chosen for their similarity to the target communities on the basis of census data and geography and the existence of organizations delivering relationship education.

The programs' impact was disappointing. Agencies delivered 6–8 hours of classes to more than 77,000 people in the demonstration cities. But a similar percentage of residents (5%–6%) received relationship education in intervention and control cities. Data collected two years later revealed that the programming made no significant difference in any domain known (or believed) to help strengthen relationships. The programs failed to improve the stability of relationships, perceptions of relationship quality, parenting stress, child well-being, awareness of services, opinions and attitudes about marriage, or peer interactions (see reference 14).

The other two evaluation projects funded by ACF—Building Strong Families (BSF) and Supporting Healthy Marriage (SHM)—provided more rigorous tests of whether relationship education programs can improve low-income couples' relationships. Both were randomized controlled trials comparing an intervention group with a no-treatment control group. In both projects, participants in the treatment group were eligible to receive up to 30 to 40 hours of group workshops focused on relationships skills. They also had access to support services such as individual consultation with family coordinators and assessment and referral to legal, employment, and other support services.

Building Strong Families

The BSF project was conducted across eight cities and included 5,102 unmarried low-income couples who were expecting or had just had a baby (average couple annual income = $20,500; see reference 16). Of couples who signed up for BSF and were assigned to the treatment group, 55% attended at least one session, and 29% attended at least 50% of sessions.[18] When outcomes were assessed 15 months after random assignment, BSF was found to have had no effect on couples' relationship stability, likelihood of marriage, relationship satisfaction, conflict management, fidelity, coparenting, or father involvement (see reference 16). There was a pattern of positive results for one site (Oklahoma City), a pattern of negative results for another site (Baltimore), and no effect on relationship outcomes at the other six sites. The intervention also offered few benefits even for couples who attended at least half of the sessions: These couples were just as likely to get married or still be romantically involved with their partner as couples in the control group, and they reported similar levels of relationship happiness and conflict management (see reference 18). Among this low income sample, there was some evidence that the intervention benefitted the relationship satisfaction of the most economically and socially disadvantaged couples (for example, those that were younger, had less education, or unemployed) most of all, but it did not affect their relationship stability.[19]

A 36-month follow-up evaluation of the BSF project showed a similarly discouraging overall pattern.[20] No significant differences were found between treatment and control group couples with regard to their likelihood of being married, marital happiness, conflict management, coparenting, or family stability. One benefit from the intervention was that their children's behavior problems were modestly reduced. But the intervention also had negative effects on some aspects of fathers' involvement, such as the amount of time they spent with their children and the financial support they provided. We can only speculate on what this might mean, but one possibility is that interventions intended to accelerate relationship development can backfire if they are offered at a time when both partners are not yet fully committed to the future of the relationship.

Results obtained 36 months after participants' random assignment to treatment or control conditions varied among different BSF study sites. In Florida, the intervention was associated with less family stability, less father involvement, and lower relationship status and quality. The negative effects observed in Baltimore at 15 months faded over time. The same was true of the positive effects from Oklahoma City, although positive effects on family stability at that site remained significant: 49% of children in the intervention group had lived with their biological parents since birth compared with 41% of children in the control group. Overall, the authors were left to conclude that "BSF did not succeed in its primary outcome of improving couples' relationships" (p. xii).[21]

Supporting Health Marriage

The SHM study included 6,300 low-income couples. Of the couples, 43% had incomes lower than the federal poverty level and 39% had incomes between 100% and 200% of the federal poverty level.[22] Eighty-one percent of couples were married, with an average marriage length of six years.

Data collected a year after random assignment to treatment or control conditions indicated the program had generally positive effects. Couples who received the intervention reported significantly more relationship happiness and better relationship interactions, as well as lower levels of psychological abuse and psychological distress.[22] Participants in the intervention conditions also demonstrated more positive communication skills during structured problem solving and social support discussions with their partner, including skills such as actively listening and openly exchanging ideas, thoughts, and feelings.

However, the treatment and control groups were similar in other respects. The percentage of participants who were married was the same for the two groups a year after the intervention began, and the groups reported no differences in severe physical assault, infidelity, or cooperative coparenting.

Results were similar 30 months after random assignment.[23] As in the initial evaluation, couples that received the intervention reported higher levels of relationship happiness, higher-quality interactions, and lower levels of psychological abuse and psychological distress. By this later evaluation period, participants in the intervention group also reported less infidelity. As at the earlier follow-up, the couples in the treatment and control groups were equally likely to be married, and there was no difference in their reports of physical assault or cooperative coparenting.

In many respects, SHM findings are more encouraging than those of the other two evaluations. First, there was a high degree of program participation: 90% of couples assigned to the treatment group attended at least one session and 43% of couples attended more than 10 sessions. Couples spent an average of 27 hours engaged in services, including 17 hours of marriage education workshops (see reference 23). Second and most important, this was the only case among the three evaluations in which a pattern of overall positive effects was observed. The consistency of outcomes at 12- and 30-month follow-up periods is important because it means the effects extended for more than a year beyond the completion of the intervention, and the fact that significant effects were found for self-report and observational measures means that couples' gains were evident to themselves and to objective observers.[24]

Nonetheless, treatment effects—although generally positive—were weak. The potency of an intervention can be quantified using a statistical concept known as *effect size*, which accounts for both the difference in the average result for two groups and the overlap between them. The average effect size from this program (0.09) falls well below standard conventions for an effect to be considered small (0.20).[25] Some scholars have argued that these minimal effects should not be dismissed entirely (see reference 24), but we note that effects of this magnitude indicate that differences between groups, although statistically different, are substantively similar. For example, the largest difference between treatment and control groups was found for couples' average reports of relationship happiness (effect size = 0.13), where the mean for the treatment group was 5.94 and the mean for the control group was 5.79 on a 7-point scale, with 7 being the happiest (see reference 23). The program also had no effect on marital stability, which was one of the intervention's primary aims. In addition, because people in the control group received no treatment at all, it's impossible to rule out the possibility that SHM's positive effects, however weak, stem not from any particular element of the intervention itself but from placebo effects.

Also problematic is the fact that the SHM program did not appear to work in a manner consistent with the theory upon which it was based. Behavioral theory would predict that changes in communication skills should lead to changes in relationship satisfaction. Here, however, although couples showed improvements in communication 12 months after the SHM intervention and subsequent improvements in their satisfaction,

the gains in satisfaction were not accounted for by changes in communication.[26] These findings indicate that changing the quality of couples' interactions did not produce significant changes in relationship quality or stability among low-income populations and leave open questions about why couples who participated in SHM showed increases in their satisfaction.

Time for a New Approach

Taken together, evaluations of these three federally funded relationship-education programs offer multiple useful insights. They show that couples with low incomes will enroll in programs in an attempt to strengthen and preserve what can be life-improving relationships. Many participants said the workshops were relevant and useful. And measurable benefits for more established couples were observed in the SHM evaluation. Nonetheless, these results also suggest several reasons why developing effective programming in this realm remains a work in progress. (Table 1 displays a summary of key outcomes for the CHMI, BSF, and SHM program evaluations.)

First, program attendance and retention were not consistently high. Although SHM had a high level of participation, attendance was much lower for BSF. The low participation rates for BSF were especially notable given that participants were provided with a variety of incentives for participation, including financial compensation, child care, transportation, and meals.[27] Low participation among this group of unmarried couples

Table 1. Community Healthy Marriage Initiative, Building Strong Families Program, and the Supporting Healthy Marriage Program Effects

Program and follow-up interval	Positive changes among participants				
	Percent married	Relationship satisfaction	More positive conflict behavior	Less negative conflict behavior	Relationship fidelity
CHMI					
24 months	0	0	0	0	0
BSF					
15 months	0	0	0	0	0
36 months	0	0	0	0	0
SHM					
12 months	0	+	+	+	0
30 months	0	+	+	+	+

Note. CHMI = Community Healthy Marriage Initiative; BSF = Building Strong Families; SHM = Supporting Healthy Marriage;

with infants may reflect a lack of interest in the material being offered or an inability to devote such a significant amount of time to this type of programming.

Second, program costs for the intensive interventions were substantial, averaging $9,100 per couple in SHM (see reference 23) and $11,000 per couple in BSF (see reference 21). Third and most important, despite these costs, the programs' effects were mostly nonsignificant. That suggests that the programs shown to be effective, at least in the short term, at enhancing relationships among middle-class couples (see reference 16) are less so among low-income populations, particularly among couples who have not yet formalized their partnerships (see reference 20).[28] Providing relationship education to low-income couples does not appear to promote more fulfilling or more stable relationships.[29]

The lack of significant effects may simply reflect what sociologist Peter Rossi named the "Iron Law," his observation that evaluations of large-scale social programs are most likely to yield no net effect.[30] Despite this, in our view, the evaluations described above, in combination with recent research on the source of strife in relationships among couples with low incomes, hold great value. Both can help inform the next generation of programs to support low-income couples and their children and, potentially, make better use of the millions of dollars that continue to be allocated for this type of programming (see reference 13).

To identify new ways forward, we draw on another oft-cited Rossi conclusion: There are three main reasons that large-scale social programs do not produce significant results. Those include a failure to identify the roots of problems, a failure to translate basic theory into programs that tackle those roots, and failures in implementation. We first apply Rossi's framework to identify more of the roots of marital discord among couples with low incomes. Then we propose alternative programming to better help these couples.

Addressing Additional Reasons Why Couples Struggle

As described earlier, much of the existing research on marriage has emphasized behavioral perspectives: Couples are assumed to become distressed because they have not developed or maintained key communication skills. Other theoretical perspectives, however, particularly the family stress model

articulated by researchers Rand Conger and Glen Elder,[31] look elsewhere. The family stress model argues that economic difficulties lead to distress among individuals in marriages, which, in turn, leads to marital conflict and marital distress. Thus, economic concerns such as being unable to pay bills or not having money left over at the end of the month ultimately lead to relationship difficulties.

A number of studies support this idea. First, financial worries create many different difficulties within relationships between people of low income. Low-income couples express concerns about financial stability, financial responsibility, acquisition of assets, and the accumulation of savings.[32] Among unmarried low-income couples, these types of financial concerns have been cited as the most common barrier to marriage. Many low-income couples who live together say they want to postpone marriage until they no longer struggle financially so that they can reduce their debt, achieve what they see as respectability, and avoid a major source of conflict.[33]

Among married low-income couples, economic concerns are also salient. Large-scale surveys comparing common relationship problems for low- and higher-income married couples indicate that both groups report similar difficulties with communication, but low-income couples are more likely than higher-income couples to report that money is a significant source of difficulty in their relationship.[34] Reflecting these unique economic concerns, low-income couples are also more likely than higher-income spouses to say that having a spouse with a steady job is important to a successful marriage.

Research makes clear that stresses related to financial instability contribute to numerous difficulties within relationships. Among Caucasian, Hispanic, and African American families, economic hardship is associated with poorer family relationships.[35] Couples under economic strain, on average, display more marital hostility and less warmth toward their spouses than financially stable couples do. They report more psychologically aggressive behaviors toward their partners such as denigrating them or refusing to talk, and they report fewer positive behaviors such as demonstrating affection, spending time together, and supporting one another's goals. In observational problem-solving and social support discussions, they display more negative behaviors such as contempt and dominance. These different factors make it so that married couples who are experiencing economic strain tend to be less satisfied in their relationships and report more marital distress than do couples with more financial stability.[31, 36–40]

Economic strain also compromises parenting, leading people to be less consistent in managing family routines and setting rules and expectations for their children, to spend more time in unhappy moods, and to be more hostile and less warm in their interactions with their fellow parent. Parents facing economic strain also tend to be less involved in their children's lives, argue more with their children over money, and feel more hostile toward their children.[41–43] These parenting struggles negatively affect children's well-being, resulting in increased depressive and anxious symptoms, as well as behaviors such as defiance and acting aggressively.[43–45]

Financial hardship also leads to negative long-term psychological and physical health among adults.[46,47] Having scarce resources consumes people's mental energy and narrows their focus to their most urgent needs, leading them to neglect more distant problems.[48,49]

Addressing Financial Stressors Could Strengthen Relationships

Findings such as those described above help illuminate why low-income couples struggle: Stress associated with having a low income undermines their relationships and their individual functioning. This shift in thinking about the roots of marital distress in low-income couples also necessitates a shift in thinking about how programs can best help the relationships of low-income couples. Keeping with leading theories, existing interventions emphasized communication skills, assuming that promoting healthier communication and relationship skills would help couples to better manage their problems and achieve greater closeness. Financial strain and other sources of stress were assessed, and couples were referred to external supports such as employment and child care services if needed. But the programs did not directly target the main problem facing low-income couples: poverty itself. Approaches that do so are needed.

We are not arguing that the psychological processes characterizing intimate relationships should be overlooked entirely in future intervention efforts. For

example, couples may need a certain degree of commitment and stability in their relationships before economic interventions can take hold. But we believe the outcomes of recent federal initiatives should encourage researchers and policymakers to look beyond these processes to the environmental factors that influence these relationships. Acknowledging and addressing couples' difficult economic circumstances through interventions that reduce their financial stress would free couples to devote time and attention to their relationships and to their children.

Social scientists and policymakers have long recognized the importance of economic strain on family and child well-being. Yet the effects of antipoverty programs on couple and family outcomes are rarely examined. After limiting our review to experimental programs focused on increasing employment and/or financial stability and excluding studies examining changes in welfare-to-work laws that did not test interventions, we were able to identify only five such studies in which marriage was examined as an outcome. All of these measured relationship stability—the percentage of participants who get married or who live with a partner—rather than relationship quality. (Table 2 summarizes the results of these studies.)

In three studies, researchers examined whether participating in a program focused on increased

Table 2. Effects on Relationship Stability for Programs Focused on Employment and Earnings

Program and follow-up interval	% married or living with a partner
Career Academies	
132-months	+
Job Corps	
48-months	+
New Hope Project	
60-months	+
Minnesota Family Investment Program	
36-months	+
Opportunity NYC-Family Rewards demonstration	
18-months	+
42-months	0

Note. 0 = no significant effect; + = significant positive effect.

employment and earnings affected the likelihood of getting married or living with a partner. The first followed young men and women who participated in Career Academies, a program that helps prepare high school students in low-income urban settings for postsecondary employment.[50] More than 11 years after beginning the program, results showed that students who were randomly assigned to Career Academies had monthly incomes that were 11% higher than those of students assigned to the non-Academy group. Their relationships also benefitted. Career Academy participants were significantly more likely to be living independently with their children and a spouse or partner, compared with students who didn't participate in Career Academies. Young men were also significantly more likely to be married and more likely to be a custodial parent. Marriage rates increased by nine percentage points (27% for non-Academy male participants versus 36% for Academy male participants) and custodial parenthood increased by 12 percentage points (25% for non-Academy male participants versus 37% for Academy male participants). Although this study did not examine whether the improved relationship outcomes were accounted for by increases in income, it is noteworthy that a program focused on employment (rather than relationship education) affected relationship stability.

The second study examined outcomes among participants randomly assigned to participate in Job Corps, a federal program combining academic instruction and vocational skills training to increase earning potential.[51] Four years after random assignment, program participants were significantly more likely to be living with a partner (whether or not they were married) than were participants in a control group (31% for Job Corps students versus 29% for the control group). Additional analysis of the same data set indicated that among young adults who had participated in Job Corps, employment and earnings significantly affected women's likelihood of getting married, but they had no such effect for men.[52] Given the importance that low-income women place on becoming financially stable before getting married (see references 32 and 33), these results may reflect women's increased willingness to marry once they have established economic independence or suggest that their increased economic success helps them attract better partners whom they are more willing to marry.

The third study examined marriage among participants in the New Hope Project.[53] New Hope was an experimental project in Milwaukee, Wisconsin, that examined the effects of a three-year, employment-based, antipoverty program among low-income adults who were randomly assigned to participate in the program or to a control group. In exchange for working 30 hours per week, participants assigned to the experimental condition received earnings supplements to raise their income level above the poverty line, child care assistance and health care subsidies, and (for those unable to find employment) a full-time or part-time job. The program's impact was assessed five years after random assignment. In addition to increasing employment and income,[54] the program increased marriage rates.[55] Low-income mothers who participated in New Hope and who had never been married were about twice as likely as mothers in the control group to be married by the five-year follow-up (21% versus 12%). Changes in income preceded changes in marriage, and changes in income mediated the association between program participation and marriage rates: Women were 8% more likely to be married for every $1,000 increase in annual income.

Two studies have examined whether increasing financial stability improves marital stability. One study involved two-parent families participating in the Minnesota Family Investment Program, which provided additional financial incentives to work, mandatory employment services, and streamlined eligibility requirements for welfare benefits. The study showed that couples randomly assigned to the intervention were more likely to be married three years after entering the program compared with those receiving Aid to Families with Dependent Children (67% versus 48%).[56]

Findings from another program for low-income families in New York City showed mixed results, however. In a randomized trial, the Opportunity NYC-Family Rewards demonstration project provided cash assistance to low-income families who met certain education, health, and workforce conditions, such as ensuring that their children attended school consistently, maintaining health insurance, and participating in job training.[57] Survey data collected one and a half years after random assignment showed that program participants were significantly more likely to be married (19% of program participants versus 16% of people in a control group). But they were also significantly more likely to be divorced (15% of program participants versus 12% of people in a control group).[57] Three and a half years after random assignment, program participants continued to be significantly more likely to be divorced (15% versus 13%).[58] The researchers speculated that increased income may have led some couples to feel more comfortable about separating, consistent with other findings suggesting that some couples postpone divorce during times of financial stress because of financial concerns.[59] Taken together, these findings call for further study of these types of cash assistance programs and suggest that couple characteristics may influence program effects.

The results from these programs must be interpreted cautiously as we await replication on a larger scale among more groups of people with low income. More research is also needed on whether these types of programs can improve relationship quality and satisfaction—and, if they do, how these improvements are generated. It will be valuable to consider whether any effects are due to increases in income alone or whether increases in income create other changes that may partially mediate any effects, such as an increased sense of autonomy and structure, reduced personal distress, reduced chronic stress, an increase in couples' leisure time together, or greater sharing of household responsibilities.

Future research should also examine whether these types of programs are sufficient to improve relationship quality on their own or whether they must be paired with more traditional psychological programs that attempt to improve individual well-being and/or the quality of relationships. In this case, increased income—through either employment or other government assistance—may put couples in a position where they are more amenable to the type of skills emphasized in these existing programs. As this is unlikely to be a one-size-fits-all approach, researchers conducting future studies should also consider what types of couples benefit from what types of services. Some couples' relationships may show improvements solely because of increased financial stability, whereas others may need programs that combine financial supports with relationship education or couples therapy to achieve and maintain healthy relationships. We note that ACF has recently sponsored the Parents and Children Together evaluation to examine the effectiveness of programs combining employment and relationship services (see reference 21). The results

of this evaluation will be released in several years and will represent a test of these ideas. When researchers are evaluating these combined programs, it will be important for them to consider whether any increased benefit outweighs the costs involved, as is necessary with all programs of this type.

Recommendations for Policy, Practice, and Research

As our review reveals, policies allocating funding for relationship education programs targeting low-income populations are expensive but appear to provide minimal benefits. A more nuanced understanding of how financial pressures affect relationship stability and relationship quality for low-income couples offers guidance on how to better serve these families. That understanding points toward several specific opportunities to change policy, practice, and research priorities in this important area.

First, we recommend greater investment in interventions and policies that improve the wider context of low-income couples' lives, which is likely to promote relationship and family well-being. We have focused here on job training and cash incentives, but other approaches, such as child care and health care subsidies, may also increase financial stability and benefit low-income families' relationships.[60] The most recent call for proposals for healthy marriage and relationship education grants from ACF included this emphasis on programs that promote economic stability and mobility and noted that "economic pressures and instability often contribute to relationship and marital dysfunction" (see reference 13), suggesting increased recognition of the need to address poverty directly.

Nonprofit organizations and counselors working with couples with low incomes should explore ways to directly address the sources of financial strain in families. Rather than tutoring couples on ways to better communicate about financial difficulties, counselors could provide resources that help reduce that strain. They should evaluate whether couples may need to first access other services, such as job training, education, medical services, or mental health services, to more fully engage with and benefit from relationship-focused services.

We recommend that service organizations working with these families expand intervention services by using nontraditional delivery methods, such as through home visits, video, or the Internet. The intensive demands of existing couple-support programs made them difficult to access on a reliable and consistent basis for many families, particularly couples in the BSF project, who were unmarried with young children. Alternative delivery approaches may increase programs' reach.[61]

Researchers can help inform this work in multiple ways. For one, studies of employment and income enhancement should include measures of relationship stability and relationship quality. Although it is widely assumed that these programs can benefit family dynamics, empirical study of these effects is extremely limited. More studies in which the effects of increased income on relationship processes and outcomes are examined are needed to test the ideas discussed here.

Finally, we recommend that researchers specify the processes and circumstances that promote healthy marriages among people with low income. Research thus far has focused mostly on the specific difficulties facing low-income couples—but the discussion leaves open the question of how successful relationships are created and maintained among this large group of Americans, as well as that of what contexts make these processes more or less likely.[62]

Couples with low incomes are at heightened risk of failed marriages, which take substantial tolls on their own and their children's well-being. The disappointing outcomes of recent large-scale federal efforts to help strengthen these relationships attest to the challenge of promoting such vital unions. Still, by incorporating new insights from basic research, more expansive strategies that acknowledge and ameliorate the financial strains faced by families with low incomes could yield more promising results. Social scientists are well equipped to assist the drive to improve these interventions by developing a new generation of research and theory that clarifies how to best promote healthy relationships and healthy families among low-income couples.

author affiliation

Lavner, Department of Psychology, University of Georgia; Karney and Bradbury, Department of Psychology, University of California, Los Angeles. Corresponding author's e-mail: lavner@uga.edu

References

1. Amato, P. R. (2000). The consequences of divorce for adults and children. *Journal of Marriage and Family, 62*, 1269–1287. doi:10.1111/j.1741-3737.2000.01269.x
2. Whisman, M. A., & Uebelacker, L. A. (2006). Impairment and distress associated with relationship discord in a national sample of married or cohabiting adults. *Journal of Family Psychology, 20*, 369–377. doi:10.1037/0893-3200.20.3.369
3. Amato, P. R. (2001). Children of divorce in the 1990s: An update of the Amato and Keith (1991) meta-analysis. *Journal of Family Psychology, 15*, 355–370. doi:10.1037/0893-3200.15.3.355
4. Cummings, E. M., & Davies, P. T. (2002). Effects of marital conflict on children: Recent advances and emerging themes in process-oriented research. *Journal of Child Psychology and Psychiatry, 43*, 31–63. doi:10.1111/1469-7610.00003
5. Whisman, M. A., Beach, S. R. H., & Snyder, D. K. (2008). Is marital discord taxonic and can taxonic status be assessed reliably? Results from a national, representative sample of married couples. *Journal of Consulting and Clinical Psychology, 76*, 745–755. doi:10.1037/0022-006X.76.5.745
6. Bramlett, M. D., & Mosher, W. D. (2001). *First marriage dissolution, divorce, and remarriage: United States*. Hyattsville, MD: National Center for Health Statistics.
7. Bramlett, M. D., & Mosher, W. D. (2002). *Cohabitation, marriage, divorce, and remarriage in the United States*. Retrieved from National Center for Health Statistics website: http://www.cdc.gov/nchs/data/series/sr_23/sr23_022.pdf
8. Pew Research Center. (2010). *The decline of marriage and rise of new families*. Retrieved from http://www.pewsocialtrends.org/2010/11/18/the-decline-of-marriage-and-rise-of-new-families/
9. Martin, J. A., Hamilton, B. E., Ventura, S. J., Osterman, M. J. K., Wilson, E. C., & Matthews, T. J. (2012). Births: Final data for 2010. *National Vital Statistics Reports, 61*(1).
10. Carlson, M., McLanahan, S., & England, P. (2004). Union formation in fragile families. *Demography, 41*, 237–261. doi:10.1353/dem.2004.0012
11. Hawkins, A. J., & Erickson, S. E. (2015). Is couple and relationship education effective for lower income participants? A meta-analytic study. *Journal of Family Psychology, 29*, 59–68. doi:10.1037/fam0000045
12. Heath, M. (2012). *One campaign under God: The campaign to promote marriage in America*. New York, NY: New York University Press.
13. Administration for Children and Families. (2015). *Healthy marriage and relationship education grants* (No. HHS-2015-ACF-OFA-FM-0985). Retrieved from http://www.acf.hhs.gov/grants/open/foa/files/HHS-2015-ACF-OFA-FM-0985_0.pdf
14. Bir, A., Lerman, R., Corwin, E., MacIlvain, B., Beard, A., Richburg, K., & Smith, K. (2012). *Impacts of a community healthy marriage initiative* (OPRE Report 2012–34A). Washington, DC: Office of Planning, Research and Evaluation, Administration for Children and Families, U.S. Department of Health and Human Services.
15. Weiss, R. L. (1980). Strategic behavioral marital therapy: Toward a model for assessment and intervention. In J. P. Vincent (Ed.), *Advances in family intervention, assessment and theory* (Vol. 1, pp. 229–271). Greenwich, CT: JAI Press.
16. Wood, R. G., McConnell, S., Moore, Q., Clarkwest, A., & Hsueh, J. (2010). *Strengthening unmarried parents' relationships: The early impacts of Building Strong Families*. Princeton, NJ: Mathematica Policy Research.
17. Hawkins, A. J., Blanchard, V. L., Baldwin, S. A., & Fawcett, E. B. (2008). Does marriage and relationship education work?

A meta-analytic study. *Journal of Consulting and Clinical Psychology, 76,* 723–734. doi:10.1037/a0012584

18. Wood, R. G., Moore, Q., & Clarkwest, A. (2011). *BSF's effects on couples who attended group relationship skills sessions: A special analysis of 15-month data* (OPRE Report 2011-17). Washington, DC: Office of Planning, Research and Evaluation, Administration for Children and Families, U.S. Department of Health and Human Services.

19. Amato, P. R. (2014). Does social and economic disadvantage moderate the effects of relationship education on unwed couples? An analysis of data from the 15-month Building Strong Families evaluation. *Family Relations, 63,* 343–355. doi:10.1111/fare.12069

20. Wood, R. G., Moore, Q., Clarkwest, A., & Killewald, A. (2014). The long-term effects of Building Strong Families: A program for unmarried parents. *Journal of Marriage and Family, 76,* 446–463. doi:10.1111/jomf.12094

21. Wood, R. G., Moore, Q., Clarkwest, A., Killewald, A., & Monahan, S. (2012). *The long-term effects of Building Strong Families: A relationship skills education program for unmarried parents, executive summary* (OPRE Report 2012-28B). Washington, DC: Office of Planning, Research and Evaluation, Administration for Children and Families, U.S. Department of Health and Human Services (OPRE).

22. Hsueh, J., Alderson, D. P., Lundquist, E., Michalopoulos, C., Gubits, D., Fein, D., & Knox, V. (2012). *The Supporting Healthy Marriage evaluation: Early impacts on low-income families* (OPRE Report 2012-11). Washington, DC: Office of Planning, Research and Evaluation, Administration for Children and Families, U.S. Department of Health and Human Services.

23. Lundquist, E., Hsueh, J., Lowenstein, A. E., Faucetta, K., Gubits, D., Michalopoulos, C., & Knox, V. (2014). *A family-strengthening program for low-income families: Final impacts from the Supporting Healthy Marriage evaluation* (OPRE Report 2014-09A). Washington, DC: Office of Planning, Research and Evaluation, Administration for Children and Families, U.S. Department of Health and Human Services.

24. Cowan, P. A., & Cowan, C. P. (2014). Controversies in couple relationship education (CRE): Overlooked evidence and implications for research and policy. *Psychology, Public Policy, and Law, 20,* 361–383. doi:10.1037/law0000025

25. Cohen, J. (1988). *Statistical power analysis for the behavioral sciences* (2nd ed.). Hillsdale, NJ: Erlbaum.

26. Williamson, H. C., Altman, N., Hsueh, J., & Bradbury, T. N. (in press). Effects of relationship education on couple communication and satisfaction: A randomized controlled trial with low-income couples. *Journal of Consulting and Clinical Psychology.*

27. Dion, M. R., Avellar, S. A., & Clary, E. (2010). *The Building Strong Families Project: Implementation of eight programs to strengthen unmarried parent families.* Princeton, NJ: Mathematica Policy Research.

28. Johnson, M. D. (2012). Healthy marriage initiatives: On the need for empiricism in policy implementation. *American Psychologist, 67,* 296–308. doi:10.1037/a0027743

29. Johnson, M. D., & Bradbury, T. N. (2015). Contributions of social learning theory to the promotion of healthy relationships: Asset or liability? *Journal of Family Theory & Review, 7,* 13–27. doi:10.1111/jftr.12057

30. Rossi, P. (1987). The Iron Law of evaluation and other metallic rules. *Research in Social Problems and Public Policy, 4,* 3–20.

31. Conger, R. D., Rueter, M. A., & Elder, G. H. (1999). Couple resilience to economic pressure. *Journal of Personality and Social Psychology, 76,* 54–71. doi:10.1037/0022-3514.76.1.54

32. Gibson-Davis, C. M., Edin, K., & McLanahan, S. (2005). High hopes but even higher expectations: The retreat from marriage among low-income couples. *Journal of Marriage and Family, 67,* 1301–1312. doi 10.1111/j.1741-3737.2005.00218.x

33. Smock, P. J., Manning, W. D., & Porter, M. (2005). "Everything's there except money": How money shapes decisions to marry among cohabitors. *Journal of Marriage and Family, 67,* 680–696. doi:10.1111/j.1741-3737.2005.00162.x

34. Trail, T. E., & Karney, B. R. (2012). What's (not) wrong with low-income marriages? *Journal of Marriage and Family, 74,* 413–427. doi:10.1111/j.1741-3737.2012.00977.x

35. Gomel, J. N., Tinsley, B. J., Parke, R. D., & Clark, K. M. (1998). The effects of economic hardship on family relationships among African American, Latino, and Euro-American families. *Journal of Family Issues, 19,* 436–467. doi:10.1177/019251398019004004

36. Conger, R. D., Elder, G. H., Lorenz, F. O., Conger, K. J., Simons, R. L., Whitbeck, L. B., . . . Melby, J. N. (1990). Linking economic hardship to marital quality and instability. *Journal of Marriage and Family, 52,* 643–656. doi:10.2307/352931

37. Falconier, M. K., & Epstein, N. B. (2010). Relationship satisfaction in Argentinean couples under economic strain: Gender differences in a dyadic stress model. *Journal of Social and Personal Relationships, 27,* 781–799. doi:10.1177/0265407510373260

38. Falconier, M. K., & Epstein, N. B. (2011). Female-demand/male-withdraw communication in Argentinian couples: A mediating factor between economic strain and relationship distress. *Personal Relationships, 18,* 586–603. doi:10.1111/j.1475-6811.2010.01326.x

39. Vinokur, A. D., Price, R. H., & Caplan, R. D. (1996). Hard times and hurtful partners: How financial strain affects depression and relationship satisfaction of unemployed persons and their spouses. *Journal of Personality and Social Psychology, 71,* 166–179. doi:10.1037/0022-3514.71.1.166

40. Williamson, H. C., Karney, B. R., & Bradbury, T. N. (2013). Financial strain and stressful events predict newlyweds' negative communication independent of relationship satisfaction. *Journal of Family Psychology, 27,* 65–75. doi:10.1037/a0031104

41. Taylor, Z. E., Larsen-Rife, D., Conger, R. D., Widaman, K. F., & Cutrona, C. E. (2010). Life stress, maternal optimism, and adolescent competence in single mother, African American families. *Journal of Family Psychology, 24,* 468–477. doi:10.1037/a0019870

42. Conger, R. D., Wallace, L. E., Sun, Y., Simons, R. L., McLoyd, V. C., & Brody, G. H. (2002). Economic pressure in African American families: A replication and extension of the family stress model. *Developmental Psychology, 38,* 179–193. doi:10.1037/0012-1649.38.2.179

43. Conger, R. D., Ge, X., Elder, G. H., Lorenz, F. O., & Simons, R. L. (1994). Economic stress, coercive family process, and developmental problems of adolescents. *Child Development, 65,* 541–561. doi:10.2307/1131401

44. Conger, R. D., Conger, K. J., Elder, G. H., Lorenz, F. O., Simons, R. L., & Whitbeck, L. B. (1993). Family economic stress and adjustment of early adolescent girls. *Developmental Psychology, 29,* 206–219. doi:10.1037/0012-1649.29.2.206

45. McLoyd, V. C. (1998). Socioeconomic disadvantage and child development. *American Psychologist, 53,* 185–204. doi:10.1037/0003-066X.53.2.185

46. Wickrama, K. A. S., Surjadi, F. F., Lorenz, F. O., Conger, R. D., & O'Neal, C. W. (2012). Family economic hardship and progression of poor mental health in middle-aged husbands and wives. *Family Relations: An Interdisciplinary Journal of Applied Family Studies, 61,* 297–312. doi:10.1111/j.1741-3729.2011.00697.x

47. Wickrama, K. A. S., Kwag, K. H., Lorenz, F. O., Conger, R. D., & Surjadi, F. F. (2010). Dynamics of family economic hardship and the progression of health problems of husbands and wives during the middle years: A perspective from rural Mid-West. *Journal of Aging and Health, 22,* 1132–1157. doi:10.1177/0898264310377353

48. Mani, A., Mullainathan, S., Shafir, E., & Zhao, J. (2013, August 30). Poverty impedes cognitive function. *Science, 341,* 976–980. doi:10.1126/science.1238041

49. Shah, A. K., Mullainathan, S., & Shafir, E. (2012, November 2). Some consequences of having too little. *Science, 338,* 682–685. doi:10.1126/science.1222426

50. Kemple, J. J. (2008). *Career academies: Long-term impacts on labor market outcomes, educational attainment, and transitions to adulthood.* New York, NY: MDRC.

51. Schochet, P. Z., Burghart, J., & Glazerman, S. (2001). *National Job Corps Study: The impacts of Job Corps on participants' employment and related outcomes.* Princeton, NJ: Mathematica Policy Research.

52. Mamun, A. A. (2008). *Effects of employment on marriage: Evidence from a randomized study of the Job Corps program.* Washington, DC: Mathematica Policy Research.

53. Bos, J. M., Huston, A. C., Granger, R. C., Duncan, G. J., Brock, T., & McLoyd, V. C. (1999). *New hope for people with low incomes: Two-year results of a program to reduce poverty and reform welfare.* New York, NY: Manpower Demonstration Research Corporation.

54. Huston, A. C., Miller, C., Richburg-Hayes, L., Duncan, G. J., Eldred, C. A., Weisner, T. S. . . . Redcross, C. (2003). *New Hope for families and children: Five-year results of a program to reduce poverty and reform welfare.* New York, NY: Manpower Demonstration Research Corporation.

55. Gassman-Pines, A., & Yoshikawa, H. (2006). Five-year effects of an anti-poverty program on marriage among never-married mothers. *Journal of Policy Analysis and Management, 25,* 11–30. doi:10.1002/pam.20154

56. Miller, C., Knox, V., Gennetian, L. A., Dodoo, M., Hunter, J. A., & Redcross, C. (2000). *Reforming welfare and rewarding work: Final report of the Minnesota Family Investment Program.* New York, NY: Manpower Demonstration Research Corporation.

57. Riccio, J., Dechausay, N., Greenberg, D., Miller, C., Rucks, Z., & Verma, N. (2010). *Toward reduced poverty across generations: Early findings from New York City's Conditional Cash Transfer Program.* New York, NY: MDRC.

58. Riccio, J., Dechausay, N., Miller, C., Nuñez, S., Verma, N., & Yang, E. (2013). *Conditional cash transfers in New York City: The continuing story of the Opportunity NYC-Family Rewards demonstration.* New York, NY: MDRC.

59. Wilcox, W. B. (2011). *The Great Recession and marriage.* Retrieved from National Marriage Project website: http://nationalmarriageproject.org/wp-content/uploads/2013/05/NMP-GreatRecession.pdf

60. Gennetian, L. A., Crosby, D. A., Huston, A. C., & Lowe, E. D. (2004). Can child care assistance in welfare and employment programs support the employment of low-income families? *Journal of Policy Analysis and Management, 23,* 723–743.

61. Bodenmann, G., Hilpert, P., Nussbeck, F. W., & Bradbury, T. N. (2014). Enhancement of couples' communication and dyadic coping by a self-directed approach: A randomized controlled trial. *Journal of Consulting and Clinical Psychology, 82,* 580–591. doi:10.1037/a0036356

62. Karney, B. R., & Bradbury, T. N. (2005). Contextual influences on marriage. *Current Directions in Psychological Science, 14,* 171–174. doi:10.1111/j.0963-7214.2005.00358.x

A personal touch in text messaging can improve microloan repayment

Dean Karlan, Melanie Morten, & Jonathan Zinman

Summary.   Because payment delays and defaults significantly affect both lenders and borrowers in fragile economies, strategies to improve timely loan repayment are needed to help make credit markets work smoothly. We worked with two microlenders to test the impact of randomly assigned text message reminders for loan repayments in the Philippines. Messages improved repayment only when they included the account officer's name and only for clients serviced by the account officer previously. These results highlight the potential and limits of communication technology for improving loan repayment rates. They also suggest that personal connections between borrowers and bank employees can be harnessed to help overcome market failures.

For credit markets to work, borrowers must repay banks enough for banks to make a profit. When banks don't expect enough repayment to make a profit, they lend less and a market failure ensues. *Microlenders,* banks that make small loans to low-income borrowers, are often plagued by late repayment problems. This costs those lenders and, inevitably, their customers. For banks, frequent late payments add an expensive administrative burden, due to the need for additional account monitoring and lawsuits, which may reduce the assets available for additional loans. For borrowers, missed payments can lead to late fees and possible legal action. Long-term patterns of delinquency may reduce their creditworthiness and ability to borrow again. To help avoid such troublesome outcomes for both parties,

we investigated a new, technology-based strategy to encourage timely loan repayment.

Our research suggests that text messaging can be a simple and inexpensive but powerful nudge in this realm. Significantly, our findings also show that some message content is superior to others, even within the constraints of a 160-character limit. The success of low-touch interactions, such as text messaging, may be dependent upon high-touch interactions, such as personal contact between a borrower and an employee at the lending institution. Messaging that acknowledges personal ties, in our research, shows particular promise.

These insights are relevant to another set of important questions in the microlending field: What drives borrowers to default? Does it stem from conditions beyond borrowers' control? Or do borrowers simply decide not to meet their commitments? If repayment messaging is ineffective, this could support

Karlan, D., Morten, M., & Zinman, J. (2016). A personal touch in text messaging can improve microloan repayment. *Behavioral Science & Policy, 1*(2).

the idea that loan default is out of a borrower's proximate control, meaning that bad luck plays a larger role than bad behavior does. In contrast, if messaging does effectively improve repayment, this would suggest that what economists call *moral hazard* could be in play. In this scenario, failure to repay on schedule relates to incentive problems, such as a borrower's decision whether to repay, not his or her inability to repay. Banks and researchers want to know how to best mitigate any moral hazard and thereby improve repayment and market efficiency.

Using Text Messaging in Microfinance

Communication via short messaging service (SMS) is already prevalent in many parts of the world where microlending is practiced. A few studies have evaluated the use of this low-cost communication in microfinance. In 2011, Ximena Cadena and Antoinette Schoar randomized whether individual microcredit clients in Uganda were sent an SMS—in most cases, a picture of the bank—three days before each monthly loan installment was due.[1] Their messages improved timely repayment by 7%–9% relative to the control group, an effect size similar to the effect of reducing the cost of the loan by 25% for borrowers who repaid in full. Karlan, McConnell, Mullainathan, and Zinman,[2] along with Kast, Meier, and Pomeranz,[3] further suggested that SMS can affect financial behavior in studies showing that text message reminders increased savings deposits among microfinance clients in four banks in four countries. However, research is still developing on how to best use Information and Communications Technology (ICT) for development (known as *ICT4D*), that is, how to harness digital technologies to advance socioeconomic development, international development, and human rights.[4–6] Studies have devoted relatively little focus to the influence of content, timing, and other mechanics of such communications.

The Philippines is a promising site for such research. Cell phone use there is widespread: In 2009, 81% of the population had a cell phone subscription; by 2014, the cell phone penetration rate was more than 100%.[7] Texting is an especially popular method of communication because of its low cost, generally about 2 cents per message. The Philippines has been ranked first globally in SMS usage, with approximately 1.4 billion text messages sent by Filipinos each day.[8]

To test whether and how text message reminders can induce timely loan repayment by individual liability microloan borrowers, we worked with two for-profit banks that are among the leading microlenders in the Philippines. Green Bank is the fifth largest bank by gross loan portfolio in the Philippines and operates in both urban and rural areas of the Visayas and Mindanao regions.[9] Mabitac is the 34th largest bank and operates in both urban and rural areas of the Luzon region.

Each participating branch sent the research team weekly reports of clients with payments due in the following week. We randomized clients to either a control group (no messages) or the treatment group (receiving text messages) as they appeared in these weekly reports. The treatment group received text messages weekly until their loan maturity date. We randomly assigned them to receive one of four different messages two days before, one day before, or the day the loan payment was due. The text messages were automatically sent using SMS server software. We also classified clients as either new or repeat borrowers on the basis of their loan history prior to the commencement of our study. Additional details about the randomization can be found online in the Supplemental Material.

Our final study sample included 943 loans originated by Green Bank and Mabitac between May 2008 and March 2010. We eliminated loans that could not be adequately matched with payment information and included only the first loan per client during this time period. The final sample captured about half of the individual liability microloans made by the two banks during this period for which the client provided a cell phone number to the lender. Additional details about the study sample are included online in the Supplemental Material.

The average loan in our study was approximately $400, repaid weekly over a 16- to 20-week term at around a 30% annual percentage rate. Microloan charge-off rates were typically around 3% for the banks in this study. Late payments were common, with 29% of weekly loan payments made at least one day late and 16% made a week late in the control group. Fourteen percent of loans were not paid in full within 30 days of the maturity date. The banks followed a standard procedure to follow up on late payments, with Mabitac beginning three days after the due date and Green Bank beginning after seven days. More detailed information regarding the loans and payments are available online in the Supplemental Material.

Can Text Messaging Change Loan Repayment Behavior?

We examined a number of variations of the text message sent to borrowers, the effects of these variations on the timeliness of borrowers' weekly payments, and borrowers' unpaid balance at loan maturity. The variations included using the borrower's name, using the account officer's name, timing when the message was sent to the borrower, and framing the message negatively (as a threat) versus positively (as a benefit). Borrowers were randomly assigned to receive no message or one of four different messages, which are shown in Table 1.

Our results were quite clear and consistent. None of the message variations significantly affected loan repayment except one: naming the account officer. We conducted two types of statistical analyses to look for effects on borrower repayment behavior. First, we compared each of the payment outcomes between the control group (who received no messages) and the treatment groups (who received the message variations) using a process called *pairwise means comparison*. We also used an analysis called *ordinary least squares regression,* which allowed us to do the pairwise means *comparison* for all treatments at once, *comparing* each to the others.

The details of the study design, the analyses, and the results can be found online in this article's Supplemental Material. To provide a more concrete illustration of these results, we include some of the specifics here.

Overall, simply receiving a text message did not improve borrowers' repayment performance relative to the repayment performance of those who did not (see Figure 1A). In both groups, an average of 29% of weekly payments were made late and around 15% were made more than a week late. Text messages also did not significantly affect the percentage of loans with a remaining balance at maturity (see Figure 1B). However, text messaging did reduce the percentage of loans with an unpaid balance 30 days past maturity, from 13.5% to 9.8% (a statistically significant reduction).

Neither the timing of when messages were sent nor positive versus negative wording significantly affected repayment. We also found no evidence that the overall effect of receiving messages changed over the time course of the loan (see Table 6 in the Supplemental Material). However, we did find that including the account officer's name, but not the borrower's name, in the message significantly improved repayment (see Figure 1A). For example, we estimated that using the account officer's name reduced the likelihood that a loan was unpaid 30 days after maturity by 5.1 percentage points (a 38% reduction on a base of 0.135; see Figure 2). We found the effect of mentioning the account officer's name was only statistically significant for borrowers who had previously borrowed from the same bank and thereby had a preexisting relationship with the account officer. No such effect was seen with first-time borrowers.

In a more detailed regression analysis designed to look for a relationship between the message variations, we found that only the positively framed messages containing the account officer's name reliably reduced payment delinquency relative to receiving no messages at all. Additional details and supporting analyses are described online in the Supplemental Material.

Evaluating ICT for Development

These results have implications for several aspects of research and practice. First, showing that repayment can be swayed by the mere wording of a text message adds evidence that default in credit markets is at least partially due to whether borrowers choose to repay or to not repay. This implies that improved enforcement strategies, such as closer monitoring of late payments, could reduce default.[10,11] Second, our results emphasize the importance of content and delivery in ICT-driven development efforts, even in brief text messages.

Table 1. Wording of text messages

Account officer named	Positive	From [officer name] of [bank name]: To have a good standing, pls pay your loan on time. If paid, pls ignore msg. Tnx
	Negative	From [officer name] of [bank name]: To avoid penalty pls pay your loan on time. If paid, pls ignore msg. Tnx.
Client named	Positive	From [bank name]: [client name], To have a good standing, pls pay your loan on time. If paid, pls ignore msg. Tnx.
	Negative	From [bank name]: [client name], To avoid penalty pls pay your loan on time. If paid, pls ignore msg. Tnx.

Figure 1A. Percentage of borrowers making late weekly payment, by message category

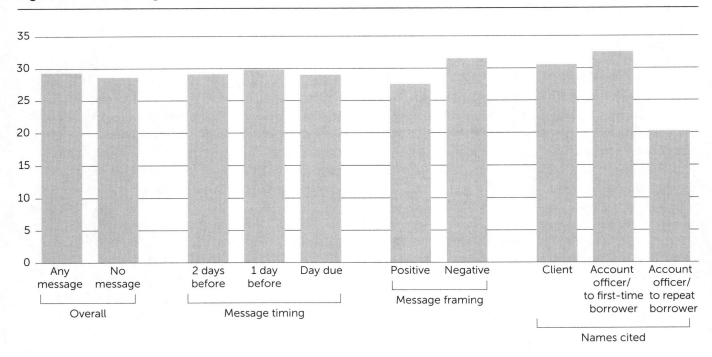

Figure 1B. Percentage of borrowers with unpaid balance at maturity, by message category

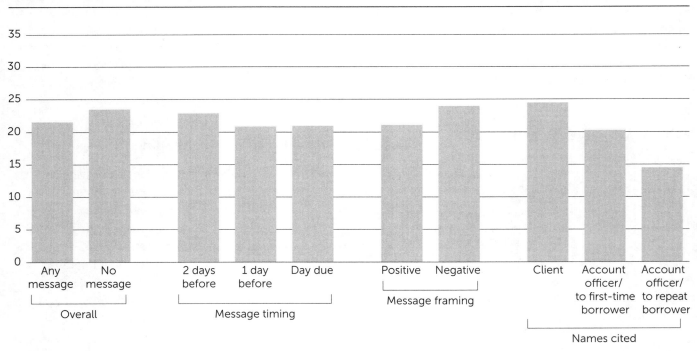

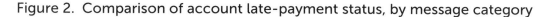

Figure 2. Comparison of account late-payment status, by message category

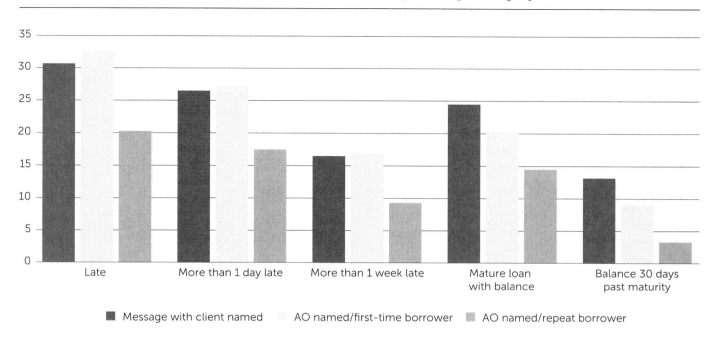

Message with client named   AO named/first-time borrower   AO named/repeat borrower

It is also interesting to consider how technological innovations interact with local institutions. For example, it seems intuitive to expect that, at least to some extent, economies of scale would favor a technological approach such as ICT in larger, transnational, transaction-based institutions over smaller, more local, relationship-based institutions. However, our results suggest that low-touch messaging strategies and high-touch interactions can combine in important ways. They also suggest that, when used strategically, well-crafted ICT-based innovations can actually support relationship lending and the smaller institutions that rely on it.

Third, the results shed some light on why some types of messages might or might not influence voluntary repayment decisions. One possibility, postulated in previous studies, is that receiving regular messages helps to mitigate limited attention on the part of the borrower (see references 1–3). Although there are some explanations of our results that could be consistent with this limited-attention interpretation (see the Supplemental Material for details), it seems doubtful that the messages served primarily as reminders because most of the messages we tried had no effect on repayment. Nor does it seem likely that the messages were interpreted as bank intentions to enforce payment. If that

were the case, we would expect that receiving any message (all of which mentioned the bank name) would increase repayment relative to receiving no message, but Figure 1A clearly shows our findings of no difference in the repayment rates, regardless of message status. Only the messages including the account officer's name improved repayment.

What explains the effectiveness of the account officer–signed messages? Or, asked more precisely, how do account officer–signed messages trigger increased borrower repayment effort and thereby mitigate moral hazard? Prior work suggests two possible mechanisms.[12,13] Work on relationship-based lending, which builds on multiple customer interactions over time, suggests that inclusion of the account officer's name may signal increased intent to monitor the borrower on this transaction compared with past transactions. Alternatively, work on social obligation and reciprocity suggests that naming the account officer may trigger better behavior from borrowers who have a personal or professional relationship with the account officer.

We have concluded that the most plausible interpretation of our findings hinges on personal relationships between borrowers and account officers. Our results showed that repeat and first-time borrowers responded to the messages differently. Veteran borrowers may feel indebted, both financially and socially, to their account officer because of their existing relationship. For these borrowers, receiving a personalized message may trigger feelings of obligation, reciprocity, or both (for example, see references 12 and 13) that increase repayment effort. Many previous studies have focused on how information acquired by bank employees can help improve loan performance through enhanced screening, monitoring efforts, or both that help banks better price and enforce loans.[14,15] By contrast, our results suggest that banks can use messaging to improve repayment without obtaining additional information about borrowers. It is important to note that this effect holds whether the underlying mechanism is providing information to the borrower (via signaling), priming a personal relationship between account officer and borrower, or both. We cannot completely rule out the possibility that repeat borrowers could view the new messages as a signal of increased diligence toward enforcement. However, as we discussed earlier, our overall results suggest that borrowers, on average, did not interpret the messages as a bank's intention to enforce payment.

Our results include some important caveats. In most cases, we did not conclude that there was an effect. However, this does not mean we can confidently say there was no effect: In many cases, the precision of our estimate is low, which means that although we did not conclude that the effect was big, we also cannot rule out the possibility that the effect was big. However, we are able to confidently state that the message that mentions the account officer by name generates a bigger effect than the other messages do. In addition, our study design only examined messaging effects on a single loan per client, and we cannot say whether borrowers may become more or less sensitive to messages over multiple loan cycles. We found no evidence that message effects change over time as clients cumulatively receive more messages, unlike other literature reporting studies that found effects that increase over time.[16–19]

Also, it is not yet clear how these findings may be extrapolated to other settings. In contrast to our results, the only previous loan repayment messaging study we know of reported that an SMS image of the borrower's bank did increase repayment, on average (see reference 1). Is this difference due to differences between the two studies in borrower characteristics? In credit market characteristics? In ICT market characteristics? In lender practices? These questions highlight the need for formulating and testing different theories about the mechanisms underlying messaging effects. It will be important to test such theories in a variety of lending scenarios with different populations of borrowers to develop a broad understanding of what types of messages work, on whom, and why.

Implications for Microfinance Policy and Development

Our findings, although preliminary, highlight several important considerations relevant to efforts to improve microfinancing enterprises. First, human interactions between the account officer and the client are a critical asset within the microfinance industry. These relationships can help mitigate credit market inefficiencies, such as repayment failures, and should be maintained even as informal and quasi-formal financial institutions become more formalized, technology-driven, and automated.

Second, a single strategy, such as specific wording of a text message, may not work equally in all circumstances or for all customers. Some of this apparent variability could be due to difficulty in defining precisely the intervention at hand; it is possible that the borrowers in our study interpreted pieces of information in the messages differently than we intended, which is similar to a lesson reported in an article by Bertrand, Karlan, Mullainathan, Shafir, and Zinman.[20] Further studies, such as testing messages with similar purposes but different wording, would help bolster the validity of the outcomes we report.[21,22]

Third, and closely related, the successful application and scaling of behavioral insights will require a more developed understanding of what works, when it works, what does not work, and why. In terms of messaging for behavior change, a key next step will be systematic, randomized, and theory-driven testing to develop an evidence base in multiple contexts and environments.[23] We see many benefits to exploring this intervention further. Conversations with bank management indicate that loan repayment improvements such as those seen here would produce cost savings that greatly exceed the cost of messaging. Text messaging may be an efficient and inexpensive way to enhance existing bank–client relationships and improve timely loan repayment.

author affiliation

Karlan, Department of Economics, Yale University; Morten, Department of Economics, Stanford University; Zinman, Department of Economics, Dartmouth College. Corresponding author's e-mail: dean.karlan@yale.edu

author note

We appreciate the cooperation of Green Bank and Rural Bank of Mabitac in designing and implementing this study. We thank the editor and anonymous reviewers; John Owens and the staff at MABS in the Philippines for help with data and implementation mechanics; and Tomoko Harigaya, Rebecca Hughes, Mark Miller, Megan McGuire, and Junica Soriano for excellent field-work. We thank participants at the 2011 Advances with Field Experiments conference and the 2013 IZA/WZB Field Days conference for helpful comments. Financial support from the Bill & Melinda Gates Foundation is gratefully acknowledged. All opinions and errors are our own.

supplemental material

- http://behavioralpolicy.org/vol-1-no-2/karlan
- Methods & Analysis
- Additional References

References

1. Cadena, X., & Schoar, A. (2011). *Remembering to pay? Reminders vs. financial incentives for loan payments* (NBER Working Paper 17020). Retrieved from National Bureau of Economic Research website: http://www.nber.org/papers/w17020.pdf
2. Karlan, D., McConnell, M., Mullainathan, S., & ZInman, J. (2016). Getting to the top of mind: How reminders increase saving. Management Science. http://pubsonline.informs.org/doi/abs/10.1287/mnsc.2015.2296
3. Kast, F., Meier, S., & Pomeranz, D. (2012). *Under-Savers Anonymous: Evidence on self-help groups and peer pressure as a savings commitment device* (NBER Working Paper 18417). Retrieved from National Bureau of Economic Research website: http://www.nber.org/papers/w18417.pdf
4. Aker, J., & Mbiti, I. (2010). Mobile phones and economic development in Africa. *Journal of Economic Perspectives, 24,* 207–232.
5. Donner, J. (2008). Research approaches to mobile use in the developing world: A review of the literature. *The Information Society: An International Journal, 24,* 140–159.
6. Jack, W., & Suri, T. (2011). *Mobile money: The economics of M-PESA* (NBER Working Paper 16721). Retrieved from National Bureau of Economic Research website: http://www.nber.org/papers/w16721.pdf
7. The World Bank. (2015). World development indicators: Philippines. Retrieved January 11, 2015, from http://databank.worldbank.org/data/reports.aspx?source=2&country=PHL&series=&period=
8. Business Wire. (2010). Research and markets: Philippines—Telecoms, mobile and broadband [Press release]. Retrieved from http://www.businesswire.com/news/home/20100823005660/en/Research-Markets-Philippines---Telecoms-Mobile-Broadband#.VhH46qRU_C4
9. Microfinance Information Exchange. (n.d.). Philippines market profile. Retrieved February 7, 2012, from http://www.mixmarket.org/mfi/country/Philippines
10. Adams, W., Einav, L., & Levin, J. (2009). Liquidity constraints and imperfect information in subprime lending. *American Economic Review, 99,* 49–84.
11. Karlan, D., & Zinman, J. (2009). Observing unobservables: Identifying information asymmetries with a consumer credit field experiment. *Econometrica, 77,* 1993–2008. doi:10.3982/ECTA5781
12. Cialdini, R., & Goldstein, N. (2004). Social influence: Compliance and conformity. *Annual Review of Psychology, 55,* 591–621.
13. Charness, G., & Dufwenberg, M. (2006). Promises and partnerships. *Econometrica, 74,* 1579–1601.
14. Agarwal, S., Ambrose, B., Chomsisengphet, S., & Liu, C. (2011). The role of soft information in a dynamic contract setting: Evidence from the home equity credit market. *Journal of Money, Credit and Banking, 43,* 633–654.
15. Boot, A. (2000). Relationship banking: What do we know? *Journal of Financial Intermediation, 9,* 7–25.
16. Calzolari, G., & Nardotto, M. (2011). *Nudging with information: A randomized field experiment* (SSRN Scholarly Paper 1924901). Available from Social Science Research Network website: https://sites.google.com/site/mattianardotto/Home/my-research
17. Altmann, S., & Traxler, C. (2014). Nudges at the dentist. *European Economic Review, 72* (November), 19–38.
18. Stango, V., & Zinman, J. (2014). Limited and varying consumer attention: Evidence from shocks to the salience of bank overdraft fees. *Review of Financial Studies, 27,* 990–1030.
19. Alan, S., Cemalcılar, M., Karlan, D., & Zinman, J. (2015). *Unshrouding effects on demand for a costly add-on: Evidence from bank overdrafts in Turkey* (NBER Working Paper 20956). Available from National Bureau of Economic Research website: http://www.nber.org/papers/w20956
20. Bertrand, M., Karlan, D., Mullainathan, S., Shafir, E., & Zinman, J. (2010). What's advertising content worth? Evidence from a consumer credit marketing field experiment. *Quarterly Journal of Economics, 125,* 263–305.
21. Lynch, J. G., Jr. (1982). On the external validity of experiments in consumer research. *Journal of Consumer Research, 9,* 225–239.
22. Lynch, J. G, Jr. (1999). Theory and external validity. *Journal of the Academy of Marketing Science, 27,* 367–376.
23. Cook, T. D., & Campbell, D. T. (1979). *Quasi-experimentation: Design & analysis issues for field settings.* Boston, MA: Houghton Mifflin.

Beyond good intentions: Prompting people to make plans improves follow-through on important tasks

Todd Rogers, Katherine L. Milkman, Leslie K. John, & Michael I. Norton

Summary. People fail to follow through on all types of important intentions, including staying fit, studying sufficiently, and voting. These failures cost individuals and society by escalating medical costs, shrinking lifetime earnings, and reducing citizen involvement in government. Evidence is mounting, however, that prompting people to make concrete and specific plans makes people more likely to act on their good intentions. Planning prompts seem to work because scheduling tasks makes people more likely to carry them out. They also help people recall in the right circumstances and in the right moment that they need to carry out a task. Prompts to make plans are simple, inexpensive, and powerful interventions that help people do what they intend to get done. They also avoid telling people what to do, allowing people to maintain autonomy over their own decisions.

That mole on Bob's arm was growing larger and darker than the others, and it had been two years since his last appointment with the dermatologist. He kept intending to get to the dermatologist for his semi-annual checkup. But when could he find the time? His team at work was short-staffed and he was juggling half a dozen projects. His aging mother across town needed his help keeping up her house. He wanted to spend whatever time was left with his wife and kids. Summer turned to fall, then to winter, then to spring. When Bob finally found the time to visit the dermatologist and learned that his mole was malignant, his most desperate wish was that he had followed through faster to see the doctor.

When individuals fail to follow through on well-intentioned plans, significant negative consequences can follow. It may seem that those repercussions are theirs and theirs alone, but they can be costly for both individuals and society. Bob's surgery and chemotherapy, requiring repeated hospitalization, will cost his health insurer hundreds of thousands of dollars. High medical costs increase insurance costs for everyone. Bob, of course, will lose income while recovering. The emotional toll on Bob and his loved ones is a particularly steep cost.

Previous research suggests a troubling fact: failure to follow through happens more often than not. In other words, people fail to fulfill the majority of their

Rogers, T., Milkman, K. L., John, L. K., & Norton, M. I. (2015). Beyond good intentions: Prompting people to make plans improves follow-through on important tasks. *Behavioral Science & Policy, 1*(2).

intentions.[1,2] People often intend to exercise and eat healthfully but don't, contributing to poor health and rising health care costs. Many students intend to study regularly but do not make the time; meaning they learn less and risk failing to achieve their potential. A surprising number of citizens fail to complete tax forms in time to meet government deadlines, forcing them to pay unnecessary penalties. Many families of high school seniors neglect to complete college financial aid forms, resulting in some students losing out on aid needed to afford college. Some heads of household fail to submit applications for food stamps, increasing their family's food insecurity. New parents intend to formulate wills and purchase life insurance but never get around to either, leading to family battles and financial insecurity when tragedy strikes. And on and on.

How can policymakers and managers more effectively help people follow through on desirable behaviors? Today, they use a combination of carrots and sticks: bonuses, late fees and other financial incentives, or regulations that require necessary tasks to be completed. But these methods can be coercive and clumsy, and they often aren't optimal for the situation at hand. Strategically prompting people to form simple plans about how and when they will follow through on their intentions, however, provides a low-cost, simple, and potent tool to complement existing strategies.

Evidence is growing that planning prompts, which nudge people at key times to think through how and when they will follow through, make people more likely to act on matters of importance to them. These inexpensive prompts, which leverage insights from behavioral science, increase follow-through on a wide range of beneficial behaviors. And policymakers can deploy them while protecting people's freedom and minimizing government interference in people's lives.

Planning prompts are not the only type of inexpensive and nonpenalty nudges that research shows can move people toward beneficial behaviors. Creating a default choice in a menu of options is another (one example is the message, "Your Happy Meal will come with apple slices unless you tell us you prefer French fries"). Defaults work because people tend to exhibit inertia and stick with the de facto option. Another type of nudge used widely in advertising and energy efficiency communications, among other realms, communicates that many other people engage in a desirable behavior (for example, "90% of your neighbors are

consuming less energy than you are per month").[3] This sort of message educates people about norms and plays on people's desire to conform to those norms.

Not all nudges, of course, are useful in every situation. It is unclear how a default choice could help people wanting to exercise more to remember to bring their running shoes to work, for example. However, planning prompts informed by behavioral science insights could. These interventions have the added benefit of facilitating life-improving behaviors and preserving individual liberty.[4] They are grounded in one basic insight: Making concrete plans helps people follow through on their intentions.

Why Planning Prompts Work

Plan making has been studied for decades. There are deep and robust literatures on the topic and on the related power of goals, goal setting, and mental simulation.[5–9] The evidence clearly shows that plan making can increase follow-through.

In one early randomized study on tetanus vaccination rates, for example, a team of social psychologists showed that 28% of Yale University seniors got the shot when they were encouraged to do so after being prompted to review their weekly schedules and to select a feasible time to stop by the health center to receive an inoculation. They were also given a list of times when shots were available and a campus map highlighting the health center's location. Only 3% of the seniors got the shot when they were simply encouraged to do so and were informed about how effective the shots were and their availability on campus.[9]

But why would prompting people to make concrete plans about when, where, and how they will act to achieve their intentions increase follow-through? Research suggests a number of reasons. Merely asking people if they intend to carry out a beneficial behavior can make it more likely that they will do it, according to numerous studies.[10–13] For example, if you ask a person who is not planning to join a gym how likely she is to join a gym, the mere question may prompt her to think more about joining than she otherwise would have, which could then make her more likely to sign up for a gym membership.

Prompting people to make a plan capitalizes on other psychological forces as well. Specifically, guiding people to unpack the when, where, and how of fulfilling their intentions can increase their likelihoods of following through.[14] In part that's because making an action plan overcomes people's tendency to procrastinate when they intend to behave in beneficial ways that fail to provide instant gratification[15,16] as well as their tendency to be overly optimistic about the time it will take to accomplish a task.[17] It accomplishes this by encouraging people to develop specific strategies to overcome logistical obstacles to following through on their good intentions. Imagine someone—let's call her Sarah—who intends to get a flu vaccination, but getting the vaccination will require an hour of travel to and from a health clinic. Prompting Sarah to make a plan to get vaccinated may lead her to block an hour off on her calendar and enlist colleagues to cover her responsibilities while she is away. Moreover, by unpacking exactly which actions are required to get a flu shot, she will be less likely to underestimate the time needed to accomplish the task—a particularly common problem for complex tasks.[18]

Making a concrete action plan also helps people overcome forgetfulness, a common obstacle to following through on good intentions.[19,20] For example, when Orbell, Hodgkins, and Sheeran surveyed women who intended but failed to perform self-examinations that can detect breast cancer, 70% of them reported that they forgot to do it.[21] Making a plan counters this tendency by helping people remember their intentions at appropriate times and by activating predetermined strategies to overcome any challenges they anticipate. It also helps people remember that to achieve their intentions, they should engage in preprogrammed behaviors at specific moments—for example, a specific time of day, when a certain event occurs, or when a specific feeling or thought arises. In other words, "if situation Y arises, then engage in behavior X."[6,22] For example, rather than Sarah simply saying she will get her flu shot next Tuesday, she could instead make a concrete plan: After she drops her son off at daycare next Tuesday, she will drive to the clinic to receive her shot. Unpacking the logistics in this way will make Sarah more likely to spontaneously remember to get her flu shot next Tuesday as she drives away from daycare.

Finally, committing to behaving in a certain way and then failing to follow through on this explicit commitment causes discomfort.[23] For example, if Sarah schedules an hour to get a flu shot on her calendar for next Tuesday but fails to get it, it would mean that she failed to honor an explicit commitment recorded on her calendar. Anticipating such discomfort probably contributes to why planning prompts increase follow-through.

Planning prompts become even more effective when they require a person to inform someone else of a commitment, such as reporting the plan to a friend or family member. Such prompts add social pressure to follow through to the other benefits of plan making.[24] Returning to our flu shot example, if Sarah had told her spouse that she planned to get the shot on Tuesday, in addition to scheduling it on her calendar, a failure to get the shot would induce added discomfort and possible embarrassment.

Although making a plan helps people accomplish their intentions, when left to their own devices, people often fail to generate concrete plans.[25] Paradoxically, people frequently underplan when they begin with strong intentions. They mistakenly believe that their strong intentions are enough to propel them to perform desired behaviors, and that belief keeps them from using strategies that could help translate intentions into actions.[26] Thus, people are prone to underplanning the behaviors they would most like to accomplish. These results underscore the need for policy interventions that encourage plan making and suggest interventions could improve social welfare.

Evidence for the Effectiveness of Prompting People to Make Plans

Prompting people to make plans can aid follow-through on a wide range of beneficial behaviors, many of them relevant to public policy. For example, college students who committed to eating additional fruit each day over a two-week period were more successful when they also received prompts to plan how, when, and where they would eat additional fruit.[27] Planning prompts also increase follow-through on other beneficial intentions, including exercise,[28,29] dieting,[30] smoking cessation,[31] recycling,[32] and test preparation[33,34] (see reference 14 for an extended review of earlier work).

Three recent large-scale field experiments described below demonstrate the power of planning prompts to influence socially important behaviors. Each illustrates a light-touch approach that policymakers might use to elicit concrete plan making. They also highlight conditions that increase the effectiveness of planning prompts.

Getting People to Vote

In the United States, tens of millions of dollars are spent each election cycle to encourage citizens to vote. Greater citizen participation affects election results, as well as which groups of citizens have more influence over legislation (for a review, see reference 35). To find out whether planning prompts can increase the effectiveness of get-out-the-vote communications, one of us (Rogers, in collaboration with David Nickerson) randomly assigned 287,000 people to one of three groups during the 2008 Democratic primary election in Pennsylvania. Members of one group received a call that featured a typical get-out-the-vote phone script: They were reminded of the upcoming election, encouraged to vote, and asked if they intended to vote. The members of the second group encountered the same script, but they were also asked three additional plan-making questions: when they would vote, where would they be coming from, and how they would get to their polling place. Those in a third group were not contacted.

By analyzing public voting records, Rogers and Nickerson showed that those who received the call based on a typical get-out-the-vote phone script were 2.0 percentage points more likely to vote than were those who weren't called. However, those who were also asked plan-making questions were 4.1 percentage points more likely to vote than were those who were not called—a statistically significant increase over the 42.9% turnout of the control group. In short, adding three simple plan-making questions made get-out-the-vote calls more than twice as effective.[36] Further analyses suggested that the plan-making calls worked particularly well on those who likely had not yet made a plan for getting to their polling place: citizens who lived in households with no other eligible voters.

To put this effect size into context, we note that a voting shift of this magnitude in the 2008 presidential general election would have changed the outcomes in Florida, Indiana, North Carolina, and Missouri. Of course, generating so large an effect size in hotly contested battleground states during a fractious general election (as opposed to a less intense primary election) is highly unlikely, as is reaching 100% of eligible voters by phone to administer a plan-making intervention. This illustration simply shows that adding the plan-making prompt to the standard get-out-the-vote calls meaningfully increases the effectiveness of voter outreach.

Expanding Flu Immunity

Plan making alters important health behaviors as well. Milkman, Beshears, Choi, Laibson, and Madrian conducted two large-scale field experiments, in collaboration with Evive Health, a company that reminds employees of client corporations by mail when they are due to receive immunizations and medical exams.[37] The first experiment involved encouraging employees to receive shots to prevent seasonal influenza, which annually causes more than 30,000 hospitalizations and more than 25,000 deaths in the United States.[38,39] The frequency of these adverse incidents could be greatly reduced if more people obtained flu shots, which are widely available, inexpensive, and effective. Past research has shown that sending reminder letters increases vaccination rates by an average of 8 percentage points.[40,41]

To see if planning prompts induced people to get flu shots, Evive Health sent more than 3,000 employees of a Midwestern company mailings encouraging them to get free flu shots at a variety of on-site work clinics. Each mailing included the date(s) and time(s) of the free flu shots and the location of the clinic at the employees' work site. Employees were randomly assigned to one of two groups. Those in a control group received a mailing with only the personalized clinic information described above. Those in the plan-making condition also received a prompt urging them to (privately) write down in a box printed on the mailing the date and time they planned to attend a clinic. Clinic attendance sheets were used to track the receipt of flu shots. This subtle prompt to make plans cost little but increased flu shot uptake from 33% of targets in the control condition to 37% in the plan-making condition.[37]

The prompt was most effective for employees whose on-site flu shot clinics were open just one day, as opposed to three or five days. In that case, the opportunity to receive a flu shot was fleeting, making failure to follow through especially costly. A full 38 percent of these employees obtained flu shots, 8 percentage points more than the control group, people who were not prompted and also had just one-day access to a flu shot clinic. These results suggest that plan-making interventions may be most potent in scenarios with only a narrow window of opportunity to act. They also indicate that adding a planning prompt to a reminder can boost follow-through by nearly as much as the reminder itself.[40,41]

Preventing Colon Cancer

In the second experiment conducted by Milkman and colleagues, Evive Health sent nearly 12,000 employees who were overdue for a colonoscopy a mailing reminding them to obtain the screening.[42] The mailings provided personalized details about the cost of a colonoscopy and how to schedule an appointment. They also included a yellow sticky note affixed to the top right-hand corner, which recipients were prompted to use as a reminder to schedule and keep their colonoscopy appointment. Employees were randomly assigned to groups. For one group, this yellow note included a plan-making prompt with blank lines for employees to write down the doctor, clinic, and date of their appointment; for another group, the note was blank.

Approximately seven months after sending the mailing, insurance claims information for employees in the study were reviewed to confirm who had received colonoscopies. Among those who had received the plan-making mailing, 7.2% received a colonoscopy, whereas only 6.2% of those who received a reminder without a planning prompt followed through. Increasing the rate of obtaining colonoscopies by one percentage point would save 271 years of life for every 100,000 people who should receive the procedure, according to a 2008 study led by Memorial Sloan Kettering Cancer Center researchers.[43] Further, the plan-making mailer's impact was most potent among subpopulations at greatest risk of forgetfulness, such as older adults, adults with children, and those who did not obtain colonoscopies after earlier reminders. This finding is consistent with past psychological studies on the impact of planning prompts and highlights the value of the prompts as a potent tool for overcoming forgetfulness.

Making the Best-Laid Plans Better

As evidence of the power of making plans has grown, researchers have probed how to improve their effectiveness. Their efforts have yielded multiple enlightening clues, many of which are summarized in Table 1. (For more comprehensive scholarly reviews, see references 7, 14, and 44). For instance, spelling out the when, where, and how of achieving a given outcome will not improve follow-through unless people have (or are persuaded to form) an intention to pursue the goal.[45] Along the same lines, planning prompts are especially

effective if they target intentions rooted in individuals' personal values rather than external pressures.[46] Plan making is even more effective when people contrast how their lives would be improved if they accomplished their goals with how their lives are currently.[47]

Planning prompts also work better under circumstances that make follow-through difficult. Prompts add the most value when people face obstacles to achieving their intentions.[6] As previously discussed, these include forgetfulness[42] and limited windows of opportunity to execute an action.[37,48] They can also include cognitive busyness, when a person's cognitive bandwidth is occupied with multiple tasks.[49]

Planning prompts are especially potent when they guide people to develop concrete and precise plans with formats such as "If I encounter situation X, then I will perform behavior Y." In this case, the plan is cognitively linked to situation X, and when the person faces that specific situation, it is automatically activated. For example, if the plan is, "At 6 p.m. tomorrow, buy a spinach salad for dinner from the deli next door," the person making the plan will be more likely to remember to go to the deli next store when the clock reads 6 p.m. Specifying the planned behavior is also critical. At 6 p.m., she will know it is time to buy a spinach salad specifically rather than needing to decide what food she should pick up.[7] Further, as discussed previously, prompting people not only to form plans but also to state them publicly can enhance the impact of prompts by layering on the added benefits of social pressure and accountability.[23]

Prompting people to plan, it should be noted, is not always useful. Planning prompts can be unnecessary, for instance, when fulfilling an intention is straightforward and easily accomplished[50] or when people have already planned.[36] The propensity to plan is a relatively stable individual attribute: Some people tend to regularly make plans, whereas others tend not to.[25] Those who tend not to plan stand to gain the most from planning prompts.

In some cases, plan making can actually be harmful and so plan-making prompts should be avoided. For example, making multiple plans concurrently may interfere with people's ability to recall and act on their intentions at critical moments.[51] In addition, planning concurrently to fulfill multiple intentions rather than a single intention can emphasize the many challenges to accomplishing those intentions. This could be

Table 1. When and why plan making prompts are most effective

When planning prompts are most effective	Why the prompts appear to help
People already have a strong intention to act.	People may be more motivated to make careful plans when they have strong intentions.
Intentions are motivated by personal values as opposed to other pressures.	People may be more motivated to make careful plans when they are intrinsically invested in their intentions.
At least a few obstacles stand in the way.	Without obstacles, achieving goals does not require much effort or attention; therefore, planning is of trivial benefit.
People have not yet made plans.	It is redundant to prompt people who have already made plans to make plans again.
People are at high risk of forgetfulness.	People at risk of forgetfulness are most in need of tools to facilitate follow-through.
Limited time exists to perform a task.	Planning prompts reduce forgetting, and forgetting is costlier when the window of opportunity to act is limited.
Planning requires detailed thinking about how to overcome specific obstacles.	Prompts help people develop specific strategies that they will need to succeed at follow-through when faced with challenging obstacles.
It's necessary to act at a precise future moment.	Prompts strengthen the mental link between a specific time and a required action so people are more likely to remember their intentions at critical times.
People are prompted to be very specific about implementation details.	Thinking through specific details about the context in which an intention can be executed makes that context function as a reminder of a person's intentions.
People state their plans publicly.	Sharing plans creates accountability to others, which makes follow-through more likely.
People have a single goal as opposed to multiple different goals.	Prompts for multiple intentions discourage people by highlighting the difficulty of successfully accomplishing each intention.
The intention does not require acting opportunistically at unanticipated times.	Making specific plans can make people inflexible and not inclined to act at unplanned times.
Intentions can be achieved all at once, as opposed to requiring many separate steps.	Intentions that can be achieved all at once are less likely to be derailed by obstacles that people cannot control.

discouraging and undermine people's commitment to their intentions and, therefore, their success.[52]

Additionally, recent research suggests that making a plan to accomplish intentions during prespecified moments may be detrimental to follow-through if people encounter unanticipated earlier opportunities to accomplish their intentions. Despite the benefits of plan making, under some conditions, it can prevent people from improvising new strategies to achieve their intentions.[53,54] These new research findings suggest that policymakers should focus on administering planning prompts for single, specific intentions that can only be executed in specific time windows.

Planning prompts are more useful for straightforward tasks such as scheduling a doctor's appointment, which requires a single phone call, than for more complex tasks that require multiple discontinuous actions to complete.[55,56] Writing a will, for example, often requires a person to collect documentation of one's assets and consult repeatedly with a lawyer. Intentions to carry out this sort of complex task are particularly vulnerable to disruption by factors outside of a decisionmaker's immediate control, such as experiencing a work or family emergency, getting distracted, or not having copies of the appropriate paperwork. To accomplish more complex tasks, it helps to break the job into smaller tasks, each of which can be done in a single session. Doing this can turn complex tasks into simpler tasks that can be helped by planning prompts. As research into this area has expanded, so have insights into when planning prompts are more and less effective, which we summarize in Table 1.

The Promise of Planning Prompts

We envision multiple arenas in which prompting people to make concrete plans could help individuals and society. For example, the IRS could prompt parents of college kids to form a plan to complete the Free Application for Federal Student Aid (FAFSA) forms required to obtain financial aid when they file their taxes, which could help more students matriculate and finish their degree. Civic groups could prompt people to plan when and how they will get to their polling place or obtain and return an absentee ballot, increasing voter participation. Doctors could prompt patients to plan when and where they will receive flu shots, better controlling the spread of disease. Managers could prompt employees to plan time to follow through with clients, ensuring important tasks aren't left undone.

Planning prompts are not panaceas, of course, and important social problems such as low voter turnout, students dropping out of high school, and health-threatening habits will not be solved with any single intervention. But planning prompts could provide low-cost ways to boost the impact of existing interventions at minimal additional cost. Unfortunately, despite their widely documented efficacy, planning prompts are not yet widely deployed.

The underuse of planning prompts may be tied to policymakers' limited exposure to scholarly research in this area. Another explanation may be that most plan-making studies published before 2010, although scientifically valid, had limitations. Some examined outcomes with little policy relevance (for example, remembering to mail a researcher an envelope on a specific date). And some used samples of participants that were not easily generalized to a broader population (for example, samples made up entirely of undergraduate students). More recent planning-prompt research has overcome these limitations and may seem to policymakers to be more directly applicable to important social problems. Although further research is needed to understand when and for which

behaviors planning prompts work best, the work to date provides strong evidence that this tool can be used to generate scalable, cost-effective interventions that help people and organizations follow through on their good intentions.

author affiliation

Rogers, Kennedy School of Government, Harvard University; Milkman, The Wharton School, University of Pennsylvania; John and Norton, Harvard Business School, Harvard University. Corresponding author's e-mail: todd_rogers@hks.harvard.edu

References

1. Young, M. R., DeSarbo, W. S., & Morwitz, V. G. (1998). The stochastic modeling of purchase intentions and behavior. *Management Science, 44,* 188–202.
2. Webb, T. L., & Sheeran, P. (2006). Does changing behavioral intentions engender behavior change? A meta-analysis of the empirical evidence. *Psychological Bulletin, 132,* 249–268.
3. Allcott, H., & Rogers, T. (2014). The short-run and long-run effects of behavioral interventions: Experimental evidence from energy conservation. *American Economic Review, 104*(10), 1–37.
4. Thaler, R. H., & Sunstein, C. R. (2008). *Nudge: Improving decisions about health, wealth, and happiness.* New Haven, CT: Yale University Press.
5. Locke, E. A., & Latham, G. P. (2002). Building a practically useful theory of goal setting and task motivation: A 35-year odyssey. *American Psychologist, 57,* 705–717.
6. Gollwitzer, P. M., & Sheeran, P. (2006). Implementation intentions and goal achievement: A meta-analysis of effects and processes. *Advances in Experimental Social Psychology, 38,* 69–119.
7. Gollwitzer, P. M., & Sheeran, P. (2006). *Implementation intentions.* Retrieved from http://cancercontrol.cancer.gov/brp/constructs/implementation_intentions/goal_intent_attain.pdf
8. Oettingen, G. (2012). Future thought and behaviour change. *European Review of Social Psychology, 23,* 1–63.
9. Leventhal, H., Singer, R., & Jones, S. (1965). Effects of fear and specificity of recommendation upon attitudes and behavior. *Journal of Personality and Social Psychology, 2,* 20–29.
10. Sherman, S. J. (1980). On the self-erasing nature of errors of prediction. *Journal of Personality and Social Psychology, 39,* 211–221.
11. Morwitz, V. G., Johnson, E., & Schmittlein, D. (1993). Does measuring intent change behavior? *Journal of Consumer Research, 20,* 46–61.
12. Greenwald, A. G., Carnot, C. G., Beach, R., & Young, B. (1987). Increasing voting behavior by asking people if they expect to vote. *Journal of Applied Psychology, 72,* 315–318.
13. Nelson, L. D., & Norton, M. I. (2005). From student to superhero: Situational primes shape future helping. *Journal of Experimental Social Psychology, 41,* 423–430.
14. Gollwitzer, P. M. (1999). Implementation intentions: Strong effects of simple plans. *American Psychologist, 54,* 493–503.

15. O'Donoghue, T., & Rabin, M. (1999). Doing it now or later. *American Economic Review, 89*(1), 103–124.

16. Milkman, K. L., Rogers, T., & Bazerman, M. H. (2008). Harnessing our inner angels and demons: What we have learned about want/should conflicts and how that knowledge can help us reduce short-sighted decision making. *Perspectives on Psychological Science, 3,* 324–338.

17. Buehler, R., Griffin, D., & Ross, M. (1994). Exploring the "planning fallacy": Why people underestimate their task completion times. *Journal of Personality and Social Psychology, 67,* 366–381.

18. Kruger, J., & Evans, M. (2004). If you don't want to be late, enumerate: Unpacking reduces the planning fallacy. *Journal of Experimental Social Psychology, 40,* 586–598.

19. Schacter, D. L. (1999). The seven sins of memory: Insights from psychology and cognitive neuroscience. *American Psychologist, 54,* 182–203.

20. Einstein, G. O., McDaniel, M. A., Williford, C. L., Pagan, J. L., & Dismukes, R. K. (2003). Forgetting of intentions in demanding situations is rapid. *Journal of Experimental Psychology: Applied, 9,* 147–162.

21. Orbell, S., Hodgkins, S., & Sheeran, P. (1997). Implementation intentions and the theory of planned behavior. *Personality and Social Psychology Bulletin, 23,* 945–954.

22. Gollwitzer, P. M., Bayer, U., & McCulloch, K. (2005). The control of the unwanted. In R. Hassin, J. Uleman, & J. A. Bargh (Eds.), *The new unconscious* (pp. 485–515). Oxford, United Kingdom: Oxford University Press.

23. Cialdini, R. B. (2009). *Influence: Science and Practice* (Vol. 4, pp. 51–96). Boston: Pearson Education.

24. Stone, J., Aronson, E., Crain, A. L., Winslow, M. P., & Fried, C. B. (1994). Inducing hypocrisy as a means of encouraging young adults to use condoms. *Personality and Social Psychology Bulletin, 20,* 116–128.

25. Lynch, J. G., Jr., Netemeyer, R. G., Spiller, S. A., & Zammit, A. (2010). A generalizable scale of propensity to plan: The long and the short of planning for time and for money. *Journal of Consumer Research, 37,* 108–128.

26. Koehler, D. J., White, R. J., & John, L. K. (2011). Good intentions, optimistic self-predictions, and missed opportunities. *Social Psychological and Personality Science, 2,* 90–96.

27. Armitage, C. J. (2007). Effects of an implementation intention-based intervention on fruit consumption. *Psychology and Health, 22,* 917–928.

28. Milne, S., Orbell, S., & Sheeran, P. (2002). Combining motivational and volitional interventions to promote exercise participation: Protection motivation theory and implementation intentions. *British Journal of Health Psychology, 7,* 163–184.

29. Prestwich, A., Lawton, R., & Conner, M. (2003). The use of implementation intentions and the decision balance sheet in promoting exercise behavior. *Psychology and Health, 18,* 707–721.

30. Achtziger, A., Gollwitzer, P. M., & Sheeran, P. (2008). Implementation intentions and shielding goal striving from unwanted thoughts and feelings. *Personality and Social Psychology Bulletin, 34,* 381–393.

31. Armitage, C. J., & Arden, M. A. (2008). How useful are the stages of change for targeting interventions? Randomized test of a brief intervention to reduce smoking. *Health Psychology, 27,* 789–798.

32. Holland, R. W., Aarts, H., & Langendam, D. (2006). Breaking and creating habits on the working floor: A field experiment on the power of implementation intentions. *Journal of Experimental Social Psychology, 42,* 776–783.

33. Bayer, C., & Gollwitzer, P. M. (2007). Boosting scholastic test scores by willpower: The role of implementation intentions. *Self and Identity, 6,* 1–19.

34. Duckworth, A. L., Grant, H., Loew, B., Oettingen, G., & Gollwitzer, P. M. (2011). Self-regulation strategies improve self-discipline in adolescents: Benefits of mental contrasting and implementation intentions. *Educational Psychology, 31,* 17–26.

35. Rogers, T., Gerber, A. S., & Fox, C. R. (2012). Rethinking why people vote: Voting as dynamic social expression. In E. Shafir (Ed.), *Behavioral foundations of policy* (pp. 91–107). New York, NY: Russell Sage Foundation.

36. Nickerson, D. W., & Rogers, T. (2010). Do you have a voting plan? Implementation intentions, voter turnout, and organic plan making. *Psychological Science, 21,* 194–199.

37. Milkman, K. L., Beshears, J., Choi, J. J., Laibson, D., & Madrian, B. C. (2011). Using implementation intentions prompts to enhance influenza vaccination rates. *PNAS: Proceedings of the National Academy of Sciences, 108,* 10415–10420.

38. Thompson, W. W., Shay, D. K., Weintraub, E., Brammer, L., Bridges, C. B., Cox, N. J., & Fukuda, K. (2004). Influenza-associated hospitalizations in the United States. *Journal of the American Medical Association, 292,* 1333–1340.

39. Thompson, W. W., Weintraub, E., Dhankhar, P., Cheng, P. Y., Brammer, L., Meltzer, M. I., . . . Shay, D. K. (2009). Estimates of US influenza-associated deaths made using four different methods. *Influenza and Other Respiratory Viruses, 3,* 37–49.

40. Briss, P. A., Rodewald, L. E., Hinman, A. R., Shefer, A. M., Strikas, R. A., Bernier, R. R., . . . Williams, S. M. (2000). Reviews of evidence regarding interventions to improve vaccination coverage in children, adolescents, and adults. *American Journal of Preventive Medicine, 18*(Suppl. 1), 97–140. doi:10.1016/S0749-3797(99)00118-X

41. Szilagyi, P. G., Bordley, C., Vann, J. C., Chelminski, A., Kraus, R. M., Margolis, P. A., & Rodewald, L. E. (2000). Effect of patient reminder/recall interventions on immunization rates: A review. *Journal of the American Medical Association, 284,* 1820–1827.

42. Milkman, K. L., Beshears, J., Choi, J. J., Laibson, D., & Madrian B. C. (2013). Planning prompts as a means of increasing preventive screening rates. *Preventive Medicine, 56,* 92–93.

43. Zauber, A. G., Lansdorp-Vogelaar, I., Knudsen, A. B., Wilschut, J., van Ballegooijen, M., & Kuntz, K. M. (2008). Evaluating test strategies for colorectal cancer screening: A decision analysis for the U.S. Preventive Services Task Force. *Annals of Internal Medicine, 149,* 659–669.

44. Dai, H., Milkman, K. L., Beshears, J., Choi, J. J., Laibson, D., & Madrian B. C. (2012). Planning prompts as a means of increasing rates of immunization and preventive screening. *Public Policy & Aging Report, 22*(4), 16–19.

45. Sheeran, P., Milne, S. E., Webb, T. L., & Gollwitzer, P. M. (2005). Implementation intentions. In M. Conner & P. Norman (Eds.), *Predicting health behavior* (2nd ed., pp. 276–323). Buckingham, United Kingdom: Open University Press.

46. Koestner, R., Lekes, N., Powers, T. A., & Chicoine, E. (2002). Attaining personal goals: Self concordance plus implementation intentions equals success. *Journal of Personality and Social Psychology, 83,* 231–244.

47. Adriaanse, M. A., Oettingen, G., Gollwitzer, P. M., Hennes, E. P., De Ridder, D. T., & De Wit, J. B. (2010). When planning is not enough: Fighting unhealthy snacking habits by mental contrasting with implementation intentions (MCII). *European Journal of Social Psychology, 40,* 1277–1293.

48. Dholakia, U. M., & Bagozzi, R. P. (2003). As time goes by: How goal and implementation intentions influence enactment of short-fuse behaviors. *Journal of Applied Social Psychology, 33,* 889–922.

49. Brandstätter, V., Lengfelder, A., & Gollwitzer, P. M. (2001). Implementation intentions and efficient action initiation. *Journal of Personality and Social Psychology, 81,* 946–960.

50. Gollwitzer, P. M., & Brandstätter, V. (1997). Implementation intentions and effective goal pursuit. *Journal of Personality and Social Psychology, 73,* 186–199.

51. Verhoeven, A. A., Adriaanse, M. A., Ridder, D. T., Vet, E., & Fennis, B. M. (2013). Less is more: The effect of multiple implementation intentions targeting unhealthy snacking habits. *European Journal of Social Psychology, 43,* 344–354.

52. Dalton, A. M., & Spiller, S.A. (2012). Too much of a good thing: The benefits of implementation intentions depend on the number of goals. *Journal of Consumer Research, 39,* 600–614.

53. Bayuk, J., Janiszewski, C., & LeBoeuf, R. (2010). Letting good opportunities pass us by: Examining the role of mind-set during goal pursuit. *Journal of Consumer Research, 37,* 570–583.

54. Masicampo, E. J., & Baumeister, R. F. (2012). Committed but closed-minded: When making a specific plan for a goal hinders success. *Social Cognition, 30,* 37–55.

55. Buehler, R., Griffin, D., & Peetz, J. (2010). Chapter One—The planning fallacy: Cognitive, motivational, and social origins. In M. P. Zanna & J. M. Olson (Eds.), *Advances in experimental social psychology* (Vol. 43, pp. 1–62). San Diego, CA: Academic Press.

56. Peetz, J., Buehler, R., & Wilson, A. (2010). Planning for the near and distant future: How does temporal distance affect task completion predictions? *Journal of Experimental Social Psychology, 46,* 709–720.

Improving the communication of uncertainty in climate science and intelligence analysis

Emily H. Ho, David V. Budescu, Mandeep K. Dhami, & David R. Mandel

Summary. Public policymakers routinely receive and communicate information characterized by uncertainty. Decisions based on such information can have important consequences, so it is imperative that uncertainties are communicated effectively. Many organizations have developed dictionaries, or *lexicons,* that contain specific language (e.g., *very likely, almost certain*) to express uncertainty. But these lexicons vary greatly and only a few have been empirically tested. We have developed evidence-based methods to standardize the language of uncertainty so that it has clear meaning understood by all parties in a given communication. We tested these methods in two policy-relevant domains: climate science and intelligence analysis. In both, evidence-based lexicons were better understood than those now used by the Intergovernmental Panel on Climate Change, the U.S. National Intelligence Council, and the U.K. Defence Intelligence. A well-established behavioral science method for eliciting the terms' full meaning was especially effective for deriving such lexicons.

Decisions are often based on judgments made under conditions of uncertainty. That is true when people answer low-stakes questions such as, what is the chance it will rain tomorrow? It is also true with high-stakes national security queries such as, how likely is Russia's ground presence in Syria to trigger a military confrontation between the United States and Russia? And it applies to environmental queries with

policy implications such as, if CO_2 emissions continue at current levels, what are the chances that rising sea levels will force a major population evacuation in Indochina in the next 50 years? Despite such high-stakes contexts, uncertainties are often communicated inappropriately, if at all.[1] In fact, the language of uncertainty may itself be a source of confusion.

Uncertainties can be communicated as precise values ("there is a 0.5 chance"), as ranges ("the probability is between 0.3 and 0.6"), as phrases ("it is not very likely"), or as a combination of phrases and ranges of numbers ("it is likely [between 0.60 and 0.85]").[2] But research has

Ho, E. H., Budescu, D. V., Dhami, M. K., & Mandel, D. R. (2015). Improving the communication of uncertainty in climate science and intelligence analysis. *Behavioral Science & Policy, 1*(2).

shown that people overwhelmingly prefer to communicate uncertainty using vague verbal terms such as *almost certain* because these terms are perceived to be more intuitive and natural.[3,4] People may avoid the alternative of precise numerical values because they can imply a false sense of precision, particularly for scenarios in which uncertainty persists.[5] For example, in the legal domain, efforts to communicate the meaning of terms such as *reasonable doubt* focus on using other vague language (for example, phrases such as *firmly convinced*), partly because using numerical values (such as *90%*) may impose greater accountability and expose errors in judgment.[6,7]

People naively assume that others share their interpretation of the phrases they use to convey uncertainty. But research shows that interpretations of such phrases vary greatly across individuals.[8] This underappreciation of variability in people's intuitive understanding of phrases used to convey probability ultimately undermines communication.[9] Given the serious problems associated with communicating uncertainty using verbal terms, researchers have suggested that people either reduce and restrict the use of such terms or develop dictionaries, or *lexicons,* that tie the verbal terms to specific numerical values or ranges.[10,11] Indeed, some organizations have used such standardized lexicons with mixed results. In some cases, organizations develop multiple lexicons that assign different meanings to the same terms.[12]

For instance, Sherman Kent, a cofounder of the Central Intelligence Agency's Office of National Estimates, proposed the use of a standardized lexicon to reduce vagueness in the communication of uncertainty in intelligence estimates. The lexicon he proposed, however, had some limitations. For example, it contained numerical gaps and it was not based on systematic research on how analysts or intelligence users interpret these terms. More recently, the European Commission Pharmaceutical Committee released a guideline for communicating the risk of side effects of over-the-counter medications. However, research revealed that the language in the guideline did not match people's understanding of the terms.[13]

With a few exceptions,[14,15] these uncertainty lexicons are developed by fiat and reflect the perceptions, perspectives, and experiences of small committees of experts in a given field. Rarely do they adequately consider the wide diversity of backgrounds and perspectives of target audiences. It is no surprise that instead of enabling clear communication of uncertainty, such lexicons can be confusing and ultimately result in ill-informed decisions. We argue that when developing a new uncertainty lexicon or testing existing ones, research must focus on demonstrating the reliability and validity of evidence-based methods. However, few studies have done this (see reference 2).[16]

Our research strongly suggests that behavioral science can help people better communicate decision-critical uncertainties. In two studies, we established alternative approaches to developing lexicons and tested their effectiveness in communicating uncertainty in two domains: climate science and intelligence analysis. Linking phrases to numerical probabilities and then confirming that the phrases are understood accurately by target audiences is a promising approach to making murky communications more precise and reliable and therefore more meaningful. In our first study, we showed that our evidence-based lexicons are more effective than the lexicon used in the reports of the Intergovernmental Panel on Climate Change (IPCC) for communicating scientific results and conclusions to the public. Our second study applies a similar approach to communicating uncertainty in intelligence analysis among professional analysts. In both cases, evidence-based uncertainty lexicons improved the effectiveness of communication for experts and nonexperts alike.

Conveying Uncertainty in Climate Science

Climate change is one of the major challenges facing our society in the 21st century. The IPCC was assembled to collect and disseminate information about the causes and potential impacts of climate change, and strategies for mitigation and adaptation in response.[17] Climate science is complex, technical, and interdisciplinary. Projections about future temperatures, precipitation, sea levels, and storm surges are subject to uncertainties associated with a variety of variables, including physical (for example, climate sensitivity), social (for example, population growth rates), and economic (for example, the cost of reducing rates of greenhouse gas emissions). These uncertainties can influence important policy decisions. For example, organizations that seek to acquire land to protect the habitat of certain species must decide which land to purchase to maximize the species' chances of survival. Such decisions rely on projections of future temperatures and precipitation in various locations, among many other factors.

Previous attempts to effectively communicate relevant climate-science results have been plagued by problems, such as increasing public confusion by not explicitly using uncertainty phrases, as was the case in the first three IPCC Assessment Reports.[18] The solution adopted by the IPCC in its reports was to use a set of verbal phrases to convey information about the relevant probabilities. For example, "It is *very likely* [emphasis added] that hot extremes, heat waves, and heavy precipitation events will continue to become more frequent" or "It is *very unlikely* [emphasis added] that the Meridional Overturning Circulation [the system of global ocean currents] will undergo a large abrupt transition during the 21st century." To ensure that its verbal phrases were interpreted as intended, the IPCC published a conversion table that assigns numerical values to certain phrases (see Table 1). For example, in the IPCC lexicon, the term *very likely* denotes a likelihood of greater than 90% and the term *unlikely* denotes a likelihood of less than 33%.

Some researchers have argued that the IPCC's conversion table is ineffective, mainly because the lexicon is not grounded in people's intuitive and consensual understanding of what the phrases mean.[19] In Study 1, we developed two uncertainty lexicons that map phrases used by the IPCC to specific numerical ranges. The lexicons are evidence-based because we developed them using people's actual interpretations of probability phrases in the context of climate science.

Constructing Evidence-Based Lexicons

To construct evidence-based lexicons in the climate science domain, we reanalyzed survey data from participants in the United States, Australia, and the United Kingdom who were part of a large international study (see details in reference 3). Participants read eight sentences from the fourth IPCC Assessment Report. The sentences included the four probability phrases that were most frequently used in IPCC reports (*very unlikely*, *unlikely*, *likely*, *very likely*) and thus were the most relevant for policy efforts.[20] For example, one sentence read, "It is very unlikely that climate changes of at least the seven centuries prior to 1950 were due to variability generated within the climate system alone." Participants had access to the IPCC's conversion table when reading the sentences.

After reading each sentence, participants were asked to characterize each phrase's intended numerical meaning in the sentence by estimating its lower and upper bounds and offering their best estimate for its specific meaning. Later, participants were presented with the same four phrases again, outside the context of sentences, and were asked to indicate the same three numerical values. (Detailed descriptions of the methods and analysis used in this research are in our Supplemental Material published online.)

For both the contextualized and the stand-alone estimation tasks, we discarded cases where a participant's best estimate of a phrase's value fell outside of the participant's estimates of its upper and lower boundaries. Consequently, we used the stand-alone estimates provided by participants (*n* = 331 to 352,

Table 1. Abbreviated Intergovernmental Panel on Climate Change (IPCC) lexicon for translation of probability phrases and two evidence-based lexicons (Study 1)

Phrase	IPCC likelihood	Evidence-based methods	
		Peak Value (PV)	Member Function (MF)
Very likely	>90	65–100	75–100
Likely	>66	45–65	40–75
Unlikely	<33	15–45	15–40
Very unlikely	<10	0–15	0–15

All values represent percentages.

Figure 1. Illustration of determination of optimal cutoff points between two adjacent phrases using the PV and MF methods (Study 1)

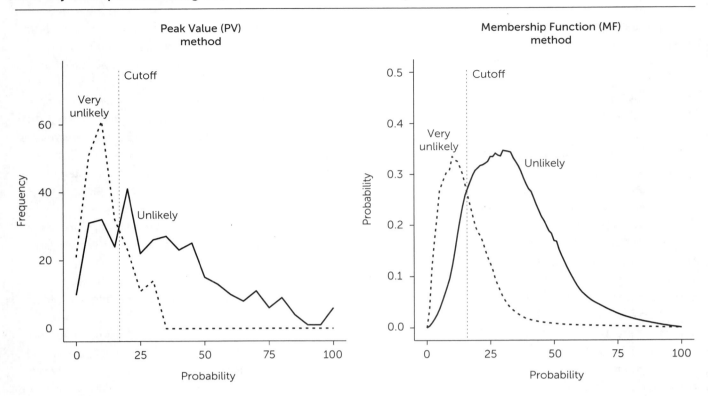

depending on the phrase) in the U.S. sample to construct two lexicons. Our primary goal was to identify regions of probability that maximize participants' consensus about the probability phrases' meaning. To do this, we applied two evidence-based approaches to associate each probability phrase with a range of numerical probabilities.

One approach, which we call the *peak value* (PV) method, reflects the distribution of participants' best estimates of the value of each phrase when it was presented alone, outside of the context of a sentence. The distributions of participants' best estimates of each phrase's numerical meanings were plotted, and we used the points where the distributions intersected to determine the cutoffs between adjacent phrases. The left panel of Figure 1 illustrates this process with the distributions of the phrases *very unlikely* and *unlikely*.

The second evidence-based approach we used is known as the *membership function* (MF) method, which uses a full description of the subjective meaning of a term. This is based on the work of Wallsten, Budescu, Rapoport, Zwick, and Forsyth, who demonstrated that

it is possible to quantify the meaning of probability terms by means of MFs that describe how well a certain numerical value defines or substitutes for a given phrase (for example, how well a probability of 0.20 defines the phrase *very unlikely*).[21] A membership of 0 denotes that the probability value does "not at all" substitute for (define) the phrase, whereas a membership of 1 indicates that a probability value "absolutely" substitutes for the phrase. A value with a membership of 1 is referred to as the *peak of the MF*, and an intermediate value reflects partial membership. The MF approach has been shown to be a reliable and valid method of measuring people's understanding and use of probability phrases (see references 10 and 12).[22,23]

Using each participant's three reported values of each probability phrase (lower bound, upper bound, and best estimate) when the phrases were presented alone, we computed MFs for each person and each term. The individual MFs of each term were averaged to obtain the sample's collective MF for each phrase. The optimal cutoff points between adjacent phrases were obtained by identifying the region of values for which the sample

Figure 2. Comparison of bounds in the IPCC guidelines with bounds from the evidence-based lexicons from Study 1

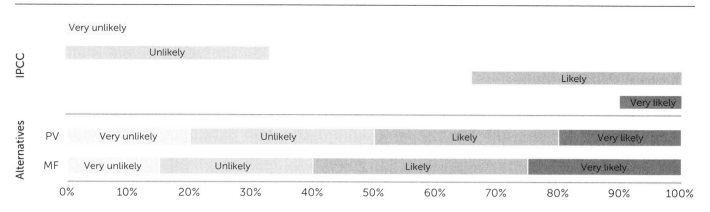

IPCC = Intergovernmental Panel on Climate Change; PV = peak value; MF = membership function. A color version of this figure is published in the Supplemental Material online.

membership of a given phrase was higher than all other phrases (see right panel of Figure 1).

Figure 2 displays the numerical cutoffs that the IPCC prescribes for each of the four probability phrases examined in Study 1 (*very unlikely, unlikely, likely, very likely*), as well as the values identified by the two evidence-based lexicons (based on context-free judgments of participants in the U.S. sample). The most prominent finding is that the IPCC's ranges for *very unlikely* and *very likely* are much narrower and more extreme (closer to the end points, 0 and 1) than are participants' intuitive and natural interpretations of these phrases.

Testing Evidence-Based Lexicons in the Climate Science Domain

To compare how effectively the two evidence-based lexicons and the existing IPCC guidelines convey information about uncertainty, we analyzed evaluations of the phrases in the eight IPCC sentences, using the responses of the Australian and U.K. samples to the IPCC sentences. We were primarily interested in how consistently participants' best estimates of a phrase's numerical interpretation fell within the numerical range that defines that phrase in each of the three lexicons (IPCC, PV method, and MF method). These consistency rates can range from 0 to 1 (for example, a consistency rate of .3 indicates that 30% of the participants' estimates fell within the specified range).

For both the Australian and the U.K. samples, consistency rates were calculated separately for each phrase across all of the participants, which yielded an overall measure of lexicon consistency. The results of this analysis are shown in Table 2. The mean consistency rates (across the U.K. and Australian samples) were 40% for the PV method and 43% for the MF method. The evidence-based lexicons clearly outperformed the current IPCC lexicon in both samples (where the consistency rate was 27% for the U.K. sample and 25% for the Australian sample), even though participants had access to the IPCC lexicon.

Table 2. Consistency rates of Study 1

Sample	Method	Mean Consistency
Evidence-based lexicon		
United Kingdom	PV	44%
United Kingdom	MF	50%
Australia	PV	41%
Australia	MF	45%
Current IPCC lexicon		
United Kingdom		27%
Australia		25%

Sample sizes in the United Kingdom vary between 162 and 177 across the four terms. In Australia, they vary between 198 and 217 across the four terms. PV = peak value; MF = membership function; IPCC = Intergovernmental Panel on Climate Change.

Communicating Uncertainty in Intelligence Assessments

We tested the robustness of the evidence-based methods proposed in Study 1 by applying them to a second domain, intelligence analysis. Intelligence analysis plays a vital role in national security and defense decisionmaking. And, like climate science, intelligence assessment is characterized by uncertainty.[24] For example, Mandel and Barnes reported that only 29.5% of 1,514 strategic intelligence forecasts with quantified uncertainties implied certainty (that is, the analysts assigned probabilities of either 0 or 1 to event occurrence).[25] In a study of intelligence organizations, one manager of intelligence analysts stated, "There is a huge problem of language used to convey probability and importance/magnitude in terms of what the expressions mean to different people" (p. 23).[26,27]

After the 9/11 terrorist attacks, there were many calls for the intelligence community to include more explicit information about uncertainties surrounding forecasts and judgments in intelligence reports.[28] The National Intelligence Council (NIC), which is responsible for long-term strategic planning in the Office of the Director of National Intelligence,[29] developed a verbal probability lexicon that ranked eight terms used for communicating uncertainty but did not associate the terms with numerical values.[30] Recently, the Office of the Director of National Intelligence updated this lexicon to include numerical ranges, the efficacy of which remains untested. The NIC's counterpart in the United Kingdom, the Defence Intelligence (DI),[31] developed a different six-category lexicon in which phrases were translated into numerical ranges, although there are some numerical ranges for which there is no probability phrase (for example, 85%–90%).[32,33] Table 3 lists both institutional lexicons. Given that the United Kingdom and the United States are close and longtime NATO allies, it is startling that the lexicons of their respective intelligence organizations disagree for every phrase in the lexicon. It is equally puzzling that neither lexicon relies on systematic empirical research and that the communicative effectiveness of both lexicons is yet to be ascertained.

Constructing Evidence-Based Lexicons

To construct an evidence-based lexicon in the intelligence-assessment domain, we used the PV and MF methods described earlier. We recruited 34 Canadian intelligence analysts who were completing an intermediate intelligence course to serve as our initial calibration sample.

The analysts rated the degree to which specific numerical probabilities (from 0% to 100% in increments of 10%) can substitute for each of eight probability phrases that are used in both the NIC and the DI lexicons (*remote chance*, *very unlikely*, *unlikely*, *even chance*, *likely*, *probably*, *very likely*, and *almost certainly*). The ratings were on a scale from 0 (*not at all*) to 100 (*absolutely*), with each 10th point labeling an interval. Thus, each participant provided 11 ratings for each phrase, a refinement of the three ratings (upper and lower bounds and best estimate) used in the IPCC study. By simply linking the 11 ratings of each term—one for each probability—one can trace the term's MF.

Following a procedure similar to that used in the IPCC study, we used the Canadian analysts' responses to derive two lexicons, using the PV and MF methods to calculate value ranges for each of the eight phrases. We recruited 27 U.K. intelligence analysts to serve as a

Table 3. National Intelligence Council and Defence Intelligence lexicons (Study 2)

National Intelligence Council		Defence Intelligence	
Phrase	Numerical value (%)	Phrase	Numerical value (%)
Remote	1–5	Remote/highly unlikely	<10
Very unlikely	5–20	Improbable/unlikely	15–20
Unlikely	20–45	Realistic possibility	25–50
Even chance	45–55		
Probably/likely	55–80	Probable/likely	55–70
Very likely	80–95	Highly probable/very likely	75–85
Almost certainly	95–99	Almost certain	>90

Table 4. Mean peaks of group membership functions for all probability phrases (Study 2)

Sample	Remote chance	Very unlikely	Unlikely	Even chance	Likely	Probably	Very likely	Almost certainly
Canada								
mean	23.0	19.4	30.6	47.9	69.1	70.0	82.9	83.5
standard deviation	31.0	25.0	28.7	23.6	24.8	26.8	17.3	23.7
United Kingdom								
mean	16.8	18.2	28.3	50.0	74.4	78.8	82.9	88.6
standard deviation	31.5	26.9	27.8	18.2	19.5	18.7	11.3	15.1

In the validation sample, the phrase *highly unlikely* is a proxy for the phrase *very unlikely*. The sample size varied between 30 and 32 for various terms in the Canadian sample and between 24 and 25 for the United Kingdom sample. Because of an administrative error in our materials, *very unlikely* judgments were not collected, and we use the phrase *highly unlikely* as a substitute.

validation sample. They performed a similar task (see reference 32, Study 1).

Table 4 presents the mean peak MFs—the best numerical representations of the phrases' meanings—for the calibration and validation samples. It is reassuring that the order of both sets of mean estimates is consistent with the implied order of the phrases in the NIC and DI lexicons. An interesting feature of the evidence-based approach is that, in addition to determining optimal cutoff points between adjacent terms, it is possible to control the size of the lexicon by changing the number of phrases used in the lexicon. We illustrate this in two ways.

Synonyms. The NIC and DI lexicons deem certain phrases to be interchangeable (such as *probably* and *likely* in the NIC lexicon and *remote* and *highly unlikely*

in the DI lexicon), meaning they can be used to represent the same numerical range (see Table 3). We examined the validity of this assumption by comparing data provided by participants in the Canadian calibration sample. Specifically, we compared the average MFs for three phrase pairs in our evidence-based lexicon (*remote chance/very unlikely*, *probably/likely*, and *very likely/almost certain*). As shown in Figure 3, the items in each of these pairs are, for all practical purposes, indistinguishable and thus can be treated as synonyms. In light of this result, we accept the determination of implicit equivalence between terms in the NIC or DI in our evidence-based lexicons.

Abbreviated Lexicons. Can a simplified lexicon containing fewer but most frequently used terms provide better differentiation between adjacent phrases

Figure 3. Comparison of average membership function estimates for *remote chance* and *very unlikely* (left panel), *likely* and *probably* (middle panel), and *very likely* and *almost certainly* (right panel) in the Canadian sample (Study 2)

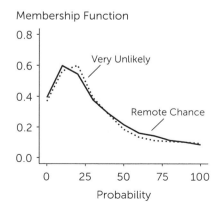
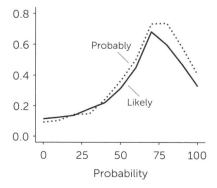
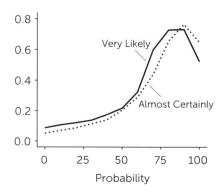

and more effective communication? To test this possibility, we analyzed the judgments of the Canadian analysts while excluding the terms *remote chance* and *almost certain*, which are rarely used, and (using the same procedures) derived a shorter, simplified lexicon.

Testing Evidence-Based Lexicons in the Intelligence Analysis Domain

As shown in Figure 4, probability phrases' numerical ranges in the DI lexicon are generally narrower than the ranges in the two evidence-based lexicons derived from responses provided by the Canadian analysts (our calibration sample), suggesting that the analysts attach broader meaning to the phrases in the middle of the lexicon than the creators of the DI lexicon assumed. In addition, the phrase ranges in the NIC are narrower at the extreme ends of the scale. On the whole, both institutional lexicons map onto different numerical values than do the same phrases in our two evidence-based lexicons.

The ranges in our two lexicons (MF and PV) are similar (see Figure 4). The most noticeable difference is that the MF method induces narrower and more extreme meanings to the end phrases (*remote chance*

and *almost certainly*), which is consistent with the evidence in the literature.[34] The abbreviated lexicon, which excludes these extreme phrases, eliminates this difference (see Figure 4).

To compare how frequently participants' subjective judgments of the numerical value of a phrase fell within the boundaries established by each lexicon, we computed consistency rates for each phrase within each lexicon. This analysis was based on the validation sample of U.K. analysts. Surprisingly, the U.K. analysts' judgments of the phrases were much more in line with the U.S. NIC lexicon than with the U.K. DI lexicon for most phrases, with the exception of the most extreme phrases (*remote chance* and *almost certainly*).

Figure 5 presents consistency rates for the PV and MF methods, both for the complete lexicon of seven phrases and the abbreviated version of five phrases. For most phrases, the intelligence analysts' judgments showed, on average, higher consistency with the evidence-based lexicons developed with the full MFs (79%) than with both the NIC's (53%) and the DI's (56%) existing lexicons. The PV-based empirical lexicon (58%) is only slightly better than its NIC and DI counterparts. More specifically, we see a much higher consistency rate for the extreme phrases in the evidence-based methods,

Figure 4. Abbreviated and optimal thresholds compared with Defence Intelligence (DI) and National Intelligence Council (NIC) lexicons (Study 2)

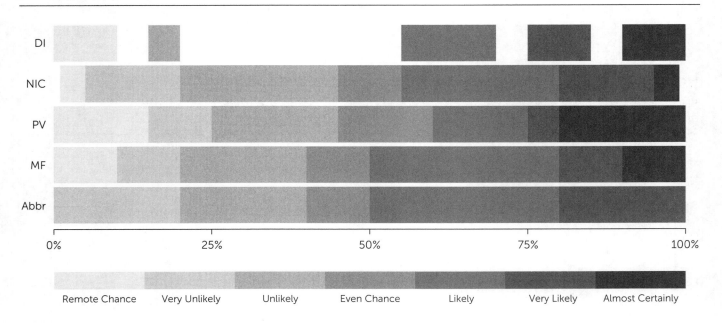

PV = peak value; MF = membership function; Abbr = abbreviated lexicon.

Figure 5. Consistency rates of National Intelligence Council (NIC), Defence Intelligence (DI), and evidence-based lexicons for the full and abbreviated evidence-based lexicons (Study 2)

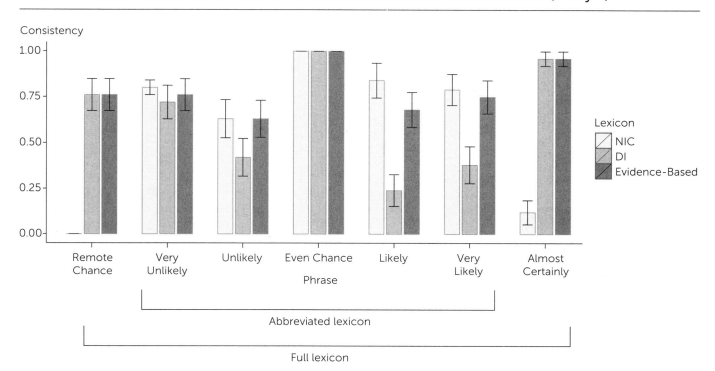

Error bars are included to indicate 95% confidence intervals. The bars display how much variation exists among data from each group. If two error bars overlap by less than a quarter of their total length (or do not overlap), the probability that the differences were observed by chance is less than 5% (i.e., statistical significance at $p < .05$).

a clear advantage over the existing NIC lexicon, and a higher consistency rate for the middle phrases, a clear advantage over the DI lexicon. The abbreviated evidence-based lexicons have high consistency rates, but the NIC lexicon is also highly consistent in this case, although this gain is greatly diminished in the extreme phrases, where the NIC lexicon is extremely narrow.

Using Evidence-Based Methods to Communicate Uncertainty

Our research shows that the current standard practices of communicating uncertainty in consequential policy domains as diverse as climate science and intelligence analysis can be ineffective. Those who receive the information may not understand it in the way it was intended by those who communicated it; as a consequence, decisions may be prone to errors and biases. Our research also shows that alternative evidence-based methods can be used to enhance understanding and the effectiveness of communication. These findings have potential implications in many other domains, such as medicine and finance.

Recognizing that the effective communication of uncertainty can be challenging, some organizations have implemented uncertainty lexicons in an attempt to improve communication. However, most existing lexicons, such as those in used in the domains of climate science and intelligence analysis, are not based on empirical evidence, and their effectiveness has not been empirically tested. It is also striking that despite the close and long-standing political and military alliance between the United States and the United Kingdom, the official NIC and DI lexicons differ in their numerical prescriptions for every verbal term. Yet, the variance in approaches is not altogether surprising, given that such standards tend to be developed "in house," often based on whatever seems to make sense at the time.

We were able to quantify and document the problems associated with such arbitrary lexicons. We also developed and tested evidence-based uncertainty lexicons, using two methods that require relatively little effort and involve low cost. Indeed, we showed that our lexicons were more effective than the existing institutional lexicons in communicating uncertainty. When people develop tools for communicating uncertainty to others—colleagues, peers, superiors, subordinates, or the general public—it is not ideal to rely on one's personal intuitions, local customs, or traditional norms. The quality of communication improves if one develops and adopts evidence-based communication tools focused on the target population (for example, patients in medical settings).

Our approach is intended to improve upon existing practices by minimizing the ambiguities inherent in communicating uncertainty in highly consequential public policy domains. We tested two methods: the PV method, which relies on a single estimate, and the MF method, which uses a full description of the subjective meaning of a term. MF performed better and its advantage was more pronounced in the intelligence application, which involves more phrases than does the IPCC. On the basis of these analyses, we consider MF to be a preferable method for developing evidence-based lexicons of uncertainty phrases, and we recommend its use. Our analysis also shows that the advantage of evidence-based methods is most pronounced for larger lexicons. In Study 2, the abbreviated NIC lexicon achieved a mean consistency rate similar to those found using our methods, but it failed to cover the entire range of interest. In particular, the NIC lexicon neglects very high and very low probabilities whose reporting to decisionmakers can be highly consequential in intelligence analysis.

Alternative evidence-based methods should be developed and tested. For example, Mandel (see reference 16) used an evidence-based approach to determine optimal numerical point probability values (as opposed to ranges) to assign to probability phrases used in a Canadian intelligence lexicon that assigns numerical point equivalents that are nevertheless meant to be interpreted as approximate (for example, a 90% probability is meant to be interpreted as "about 90%"; see also reference 13). Whereas lexicons with mutually exclusive and exhaustive range equivalents offer communicators the opportunity to convey any probability level, lexicons with point equivalents provide end users with more precise estimates of uncertainty.

It is important to recognize that there is no universal lexicon (see, for example, the ranges associated with the phrase *very likely* in Tables 1 and 3). The ranges depend on several factors, such as the number of terms used, the specific evidence-based method used (we see slight differences between the MF and PV methods), and the presence or absence of anchor terms at the two ends of the scale and at its center. The content of an effective lexicon may also be sensitive to its specific application. For example, a regulatory agency that seeks to develop a scale to communicate the likelihood of side effects associated with different drugs may find that *unlikely* is interpreted differently when the drug is a simple over-the-counter pain reliever compared to when it is an experimental treatment for a life-threatening condition (see reference 8).[35] It is best to derive application-specific lexicons that are tailored to the specific needs of any given domain and the expected level of precision.

Evidence-based methods do not completely eliminate the possibility of miscommunication. For example, recipients of probabilistic information tend to discount it somewhat and interpret it as less extreme than intended by communicators (see reference 8). Also, people typically process new information through the lens of their attitudes and beliefs. For example, Budescu, Por, and Broomell documented different interpretations of communications about climate science as a function of the recipients' ideology, attitudes toward the environment, and political affiliation (see reference 19). Indeed, research[36,37] has shown that probability phrases are subject to bias and distortion that fits one's expected and preferred conclusions (known as *motivated reasoning*).[38] However, the possibility of miscommunication is not fully eliminated by using numerical terms because the interpretation of numerical quantifiers is itself often imprecise and contextually dependent.[39] For instance, a point value, X, may be interpreted as lower ("at least X") or upper bound ("at most X"), as approximate ("about X"), or as precise ("exactly X").

Applying New Insights into Communicating Uncertainty

We recommend that behavioral science be used routinely in efforts to develop evidence-based tools for communicating uncertainty. In some domains, such as intelligence analysis, there has been longstanding opposition to quantifying uncertainty (see references

14, 24, and 28).[40] Empirical methods can delineate the limitations of existing approaches and offer sensible solutions to remedy them. The MF method, which elicited participants' full understanding of the key terms, was especially effective. In Study 1, we showed that the general public has a broader interpretation of probability phrases than the IPCC intended with its lexicon, and, in Study 2, we found that intelligence analysts' conceptions of probability terms simply do not match those of the organizational lexicons we examined. Moreover, we found that the U.S. and U.K. lexicons were inconsistent with each other, a factor that could undermine shared situational awareness and interoperability in allied military operations. Applying similar empirical verification processes to other domains, such as public health and finance, may reveal similar discrepancies in intended message and actual audience understanding, which opens the door to finding ways to increase communicative effectiveness.

When the nature and quality of the available evidence does not justify exclusive use of numerical communications, we recommend that probability phrases and numerical values be combined (see reference 2). This approach is sensitive to different people's preferences, and it also has the flexibility of adjusting the range of values in some cases to signal more precision. For example, in the context of an IPCC report, *very likely* may generally mean a probability greater than 85%, but in special cases, the communicator may feel sufficiently confident to say that the event is *very likely* but combine it with a more precise numerical meaning, say, between 90% and 95%.

Miscommunication is fertile ground for blame in public and private spheres. Organizations that inform policymakers about topics featuring uncertainty routinely get blamed when things go wrong. Ultimately, an evidence-based approach to communicating uncertainty would improve organizational accountability in such scenarios.[41] Let's face it: Uncertainty will never disappear. The job of expert assessors, such as intelligence analysts, is not to eliminate uncertainties but to assess them as accurately as possible.[42] Given that uncertainties are ubiquitous in the thorny issues that policymakers grapple with, it is incumbent on expert communities to use all effective means at their disposal to improve how they communicate such uncertainties. Evidence-based methods for doing so are their best bet.

author note

Portions of this research were funded by Grants 1049208 and 1125879 from the U.S. National Science Foundation, the Defence Research and Development Canada Joint Intelligence Collection and Analytic Capability Project, and Her Majesty's Government. This research contributes to the NATO System Analysis and Studies Panel Technical Team on Assessment and Communication of Risk and Uncertainty to Support Decision-Making (SAS-114). We thank Thomas S. Wallsten, professor emeritus at the University of Maryland, College Park, for useful feedback on the manuscript, and Ronald Wulf, formerly of the Canadian Forces School of Military Intelligence, for facilitating the data collection from the Canadian sample in Study 2. Copyright of this article belongs to Her Majesty the Queen in Right of Canada, as represented by Defence Research and Development Canada.

author affiliation

Ho, and Budescu, Department of Psychology, Fordham University; Dhami, Department of Psychology, Middlesex University; and Mandel, Socio-Cognitive Systems Section, Toronto Research Centre, Defence Research and Development Canada. Corresponding author's e-mail: eho2@fordham.edu

supplemental material

- http://behavioralpolicy.org/vol-1-no-2/ho
- Methods & Analysis
- Additional References

References

1. Morgan, M. G., Henrion, M., & Small, M. (1990). *Uncertainty: A guide to dealing with uncertainty in quantitative risk and policy analysis.* Cambridge, United Kingdom: Cambridge University Press.
2. Budescu, D. V., Por, H.-H., Broomell, S. B., & Smithson, M. (2014). The interpretation of IPCC probabilistic statements around the world. *Nature Climate Change, 4,* 508–512. doi:10.1038/nclimate2194
3. Brun, W., & Teigen, K. H. (1988). Verbal probabilities: Ambiguous, context dependent, or both? *Organizational Behavior and Human Decision Processes, 41,* 390–404
4. Wallsten, T. S., Budescu, D. V., Zwick, R., & Kemp, S. M. (1993). Preferences and reasons for communicating probabilistic information in numeric or verbal terms. *Bulletin of the Psychonomic Society, 31,* 135–138. doi:10.3758/BF03334162

5. Fox, C. R., & Ülkümen, G. (2011). Distinguishing two dimensions of uncertainty. In W. Brun, G. Keren, G. Kirkeboen, & H. Montgomery (Eds.), *Perspectives on thinking, judging and decision making* (pp. 21–35). Oslo, Norway: Univeristetforlaget.

6. Dhami, M. K. (2008). On measuring quantitative interpretations of reasonable doubt. *Journal of Experimental Psychology: Applied, 14*, 353–363. doi:10.1037/a0013344

7. Dhami, M. K., Lundrigan, S., & Mueller-Johnson, K. (2015). Instructions on reasonable doubt: Defining the standard of proof and the juror's task. *Psychology, Public Policy, and Law, 21*, 169–178.

8. Wallsten, T. S., & Budescu, D. V. (1995). A review of human linguistic probability processing: General principles and empirical evidence. *The Knowledge Engineering Review, 10*, 43–62. doi:10.1017/S0269888900007256

9. Budescu, D. V., & Wallsten, T. S. (1985). Consistency in interpretation of probabilistic phrases. *Organizational Behavior and Human Decision Processes, 36*, 391–405. doi:10.1016/0749-5978(85)90007-X

10. Karelitz, T. M., & Budescu, D. V. (2004). You say "probable" and I say "likely": Improving interpersonal communication with verbal probability phrases. *Journal of Experimental Psychology: Applied, 10*, 25–41. doi:10.1037/1076-898X.10.1.25

11. Dhami, M., & Wallsten, T. S. (2005). Interpersonal comparison of subjective probabilities: Toward translating linguistic probabilities. *Memory & Cognition, 33*, 1057–1068. doi:10.3758/BF03193213

12. Mandel, D. R. (2007). *Toward a concept of risk for effective military decision making* (Technical Report 2007-124). Retrieved from Defence Research and Development Canada website: http://cradpdf.drdc-rddc.gc.ca/PDFS/unc68/p529014.pdf

13. Berry, D., Raynor, D. K., Knapp, P., & Bersellini, E. (2003). Patients' understanding of risk associated with medication use: Impact of European Commission guidelines and other risk scales. *Drug Safety, 26*, 1–11. doi:10.2165/00002018-200326010-00001

14. Barnes, A. (2015). Making intelligence analysis more intelligent: Using numeric probabilities. *Intelligence and National Security.* Advance online publication. doi:10.1080/02684527.2014.994955

15. Mosteller, F., & Youtz, C. (1990). Quantifying probabilistic expressions. *Statistical Science, 5*, 2–16.

16. Mandel, D. R. (2015). Accuracy of intelligence forecasts from the intelligence consumer's perspective. *Policy Insights from the Behavioral and Brain Sciences, 2*, 111–120.

17. Intergovernmental Panel on Climate Change. (n.d.). Organization. Retrieved December 13, 2015, from http://www.ipcc.ch/organization/organization.shtml

18. Swart, R., Bernstein, L., Ha-Duong, M., & Petersen, A. (2009). Agreeing to disagree: Uncertainty management in assessing climate change, impacts and responses by the IPCC. *Climatic Change, 92*, 1–29.

19. Budescu, D. V., Por, H. H., & Broomell, S. B. (2012). Effective communication of uncertainty in the IPCC reports. *Climatic Change, 113*, 181–200.

20. Ha-Duong, M., Swart, R., Bernstein, L., & Petersen, R. (2007). Uncertainty management in the IPCC: Agreeing to disagree. *Global Environmental Change, 17*, 8–11. doi:10.1007/s10584-008-9444-7

21. Wallsten, T. S., Budescu, D. V., Rapoport, A., Zwick, R., & Forsyth, B. (1986). Measuring the vague meaning of probability terms. *Journal of Experimental Psychology: General, 115*, 348–365. doi:10.1037/0096-3445.115.4.348

22. Dhami, M. K. (2008). On measuring quantitative interpretations of reasonable doubt. *Journal of Experimental Psychology: Applied, 14*, 353–363.

23. Lundrigan, S., Dhami, M. K., & Mueller-Johnson, K. (2013). Predicting verdicts using pre-trial attitudes and standard of proof. *Legal and Criminological Psychology.* Advance online publication. doi:10.1111/lcrp.12043

24. Kent, S. (1964). *Words of estimative probability.* Retrieved from Central Intelligence Agency website: https://www.cia.gov/library/center-for-the-study-of-intelligence/csi-publications/books-and-monographs/sherman-kent-and-the-board-of-national-estimates-collected-essays/6words.html

25. Mandel, D. R., & Barnes, A. (2014). Accuracy of forecasts in strategic intelligence. *Proceedings of the National Academy of Sciences, USA, 111*, 10984–10989. doi:10.1073/pnas.1406138111

26. Derbentseva, N., McLellan, L., & Mandel, D. R. (2010). *Issues in intelligence production: Summary of interviews with Canadian managers of intelligence analysts* (Technical Report 2010-144). Retrieved from Defence Research and Development Canada website: http://pubs.drdc-rddc.gc.ca/PDFS/unc111/p534903_A1b.pdf

27. Adams, B. A., Thomson, M., Derbentseva, N., & Mandel, D. R. (2012). *Capability challenges in the human domain for intelligence analysis: Report on community-wide discussions with Canadian intelligence professionals* (Contract Report 2011-182). Retrieved from the Defence Research and Development Canada website: http://pubs.drdc-rddc.gc.ca/PDFS/unc118/p536570_A1b.pdf

28. Weiss, C. (2007). Communicating uncertainty in intelligence and other professions. *International Journal of Intelligence and CounterIntelligence, 21*, 57–85. doi:10.1080/08850600701649312

29. Office of the Director of National Intelligence. (n.d.). National Intelligence Council. Retrieved December 14, 2015, from http://www.dni.gov/index.php/about/organization/national-intelligence-council-who-we-are

30. National Intelligence Council. (2007). *Prospects for Iraq's stability: A challenging road ahead.* Retrieved from http://fas.org/irp/dni/iraq020207.pdf

31. Gov.UK. (n.d.). Defence Intelligence. Retrieved December 14, 2015, from https://www.gov.uk/government/groups/defence-intelligence

32. Dhami, M. K. (2013). *Understanding and communicating uncertainty in intelligence analysis.* Unclassified report prepared for Her Majesty's Government, United Kingdom. (Available from the author).

33. Defence Intelligence. (n.d). *Quick wins for busy analysts.* London, United Kingdom: United Kingdom Ministry of Defence.

34. Budescu, D. V., Karelitz, T. M., & Wallsten, T. S. (2003). Predicting the directionality of probability phrases from their membership functions. *Journal of Behavioral Decision Making, 16*, 159–180.

35. Harris, A. J. L., & Corner, A. (2011). Communicating environmental risks: Clarifying the severity effect in interpretations of verbal probability expressions. *Journal of Experimental Psychology: Learning, Memory, and Cognition, 37*, 1571–1578.

36. Fox, C. R., & Irwin, J. R. (1998). The role of context in the communication of uncertain beliefs. *Basic and Applied Social Psychology, 20,* 57–70.

37. Piercey, M. D. (2009). Motivated reasoning and verbal vs. numerical probability assessment: Evidence from an accounting context. *Organizational Behavior and Human Decision Processes, 108,* 330–341. doi:10.1016/j.obhdp.2008.05.004

38. Kunda, Z. (1990). The case for motivated reasoning. *Psychological Bulletin, 108,* 480–498.

39. Mandel, D. R. (2015). Communicating numeric quantities in context: Implications for decision science and rationality claims. *Frontiers in Psychology, 6,* Article 537. doi:10.3389/fpsyg.2015.00537

40. Mandel, D. R., Barnes, A., & Richards, K. (2014). *A quantitative assessment of the quality of strategic intelligence forecasts* (Technical Report 2013-036). Retrieved from the Defence Research and Development Canada website: http://cradpdf.drdc-rddc.gc.ca/PDFS/unc142/p538628_A1b.pdf

41. Dhami, M. K., Mandel, D. R., Mellers, B., & Tetlock, P. (2015). Improving intelligence analysis with decision science. *Perspectives on Psychological Science, 106,* 753–757.

42. Friedman, J. A., & Zeckhauser, R. (2012). Assessing uncertainty in intelligence. *Intelligence and National Security, 27,* 824–847.

Moving citizens online: Using salience & message framing to motivate behavior change

Noah Castelo, Elizabeth Hardy, Julian House, Nina Mazar, Claire Tsai, & Min Zhao

Summary. To improve efficiency and reduce costs, government agencies provide more and more services online. Yet, sometimes people do not access these new services. For example, prior to our field experiment intervention, Ontario spent $35 million annually on infrastructure needed for in-person license plate sticker renewals. In Canada's most populous province, only 10% of renewals occurred online. Our intervention tested variations in messaging mailed with sticker renewal forms that encouraged consumers to renew online. We changed text and color on the envelope to try to make the benefits of the online service more salient. In addition, changes to text and color on the renewal form itself emphasized either consumer gains from online renewals or losses associated with in-person renewals. Each intervention increased use of the online service when compared to the unaltered messaging. The combination of salience and gain framing achieved the highest number of online renewals: a 41.7% relative increase.

It would be impossible to inventory all of the useful transactions people conduct on the Internet every single day. In 2014 alone, e-retailers based in the United States sold more than $300 billion of merchandise, according to the U.S. Department of Commerce.[1] But valuable online activity includes much more than shopping. Most U.S. colleges and universities offer online courses, for example. People commonly publish books,

raise money for deserving charities, and even find life partners online.

Governments, however, are not always as successful at convincing citizens to access public services online. For example, in a 2012 nationally representative survey, the majority (52%) of Canadians reported that they never or only sometimes access government services online, despite the fact that 84% in the same survey expressed interest in using such e-services.[2] This is a missed opportunity, because conducting government business online, when done well, can cut costs and increase efficiency as well as consumer satisfaction.

Castelo, N., Hardy, E., House, J., Mazar, N., Tsai, C., & Zhao, M. (2015). Moving citizens online: Using salience & message framing to motivate behavior change. *Behavioral Science & Policy, 1*(2).

In Ontario, Canada's most populous province, the provincial government has made more than 40 services available online, including address changes, driver's license and health card renewals, and copy requests for various records such as birth and marriage certificates. Expanding citizens' use of just one online service, the annual or biennial renewal of automobile license plates, could potentially save millions of dollars. Since 2010, Ontarians have been able to go online to renew the stickers that display when their license plate fees expire. But as of 2013, only 10% of these transactions were conducted digitally. Servicing the remaining 90% of renewals in-person cost over $35 million that year; online renewals are accomplished for a fraction of that cost.

Efforts to fix such discrepancies can benefit from insights produced by researchers in the field of behavioral science, who have expertise in developing and testing methods that help people accomplish behavioral change. Beginning in 2013, we applied our expertise in a first-of-its-kind collaboration between Ontario's Behavioural Insights Unit (BIU) and the Behavioural Economics in Action research hub (BEAR) at the Rotman School of Management of the University of Toronto. The results were promising. Not only did we increase online license plate sticker renewals in Ontario, but there is also evidence that our interventions increased the number of on-time renewals, too. These findings suggest that no-cost interventions such as those we tested can save a provincial government money and help citizens in ways beyond providing convenience. By renewing their stickers on time, vehicle owners avoid incurring citations and fines. At the same time, police forces potentially gain time to focus on more pressing enforcement matters.

Using Choice Architecture to Change Behavior

People frequently face a major challenge when it comes to acting on their good intentions. Behavioral scientists call this the *last-mile problem*.[3] People who plan to save often put away less money than they need later, for example.[4] People who fully believe in the importance of a good cause end up not donating to that cause.[5] To help people to act on their good intentions, governments are increasingly applying behavioral science insights.[6,7] One of the most successful approaches to helping people act on their intentions is to carefully

design the *choice architecture* (that is, the way in which options are presented or preferences are elicited) in ways that nudge people to make desirable decisions while preserving their freedom of choice.[8] For example, people tend to view outcomes in terms of losses and gains relative to context-dependent reference points, such as when they compare an existing investment portfolio's worth with its maximum and minimum potential value. What is more, people are about twice as sensitive to differences framed as losses compared with the same differences framed as gains, a phenomenon known as *loss aversion*.[9–11]

In another example, partially due to loss aversion, the default option among a group of options tends to be "sticky." That is, people are reluctant to give up a default because the losses inherent in doing so often subjectively outweigh the relative gains of alternative options. Accordingly, defaults have been shown to exert a strong influence on choices, even those as consequential as whether to become an organ donor[12] or whether to enroll in a 401(k) retirement savings plan.[13]

Choice architecture interventions make use of such insights to help people make better decisions. For instance, informing people that the majority of citizens pay their taxes on time (communicating a descriptive social norm) led to a 15% increase in the percentage of British citizens who paid their overdue taxes in 2011 and 2012. During a 23-day experiment involving just 100,000 taxpayers, this resulted in an additional £9 million in government revenue. It has been estimated that this intervention could bring in approximately £160 million at very low cost when implemented countrywide.[14,15] In a different field experiment, 6,824 insurance policy holders in the United States were asked to endorse the statement "I promise that the information I am providing is true" with their signature at the top rather than at the bottom of an audit form before self-reporting their cars' odometer mileage. This precommitment to truthfulness (acting as moral reminder) significantly reduced the extent of dishonest self-reports, resulting in an estimated additional $1 million in insurance premium revenue over a 24-month period.[16] Even subtle cues in a physical choice environment, such as queue guides and area carpets, can create the feeling that it is almost one's turn and therefore increase the likelihood that consumers will stay in line rather than leave the queue.[17]

Leveraging Research on What Motivates People to Act

In our field experiment, we attempted to nudge more citizens of Ontario to renew their license plate stickers online rather than doing so in-person at ServiceOntario centers. These stickers need to be attached to vehicle license plates to show that owners have paid the required fees. Vehicle owners can choose to renew for one or two years, with no discount for renewing for two. The fees for renewing online are the same as those people pay when renewing in-person at ServiceOntario centers.

We tested three interventions that were developed using insights from two areas of behavioral science research. One body of work demonstrates the importance of *salience,* the degree to which something grabs a person's attention. The other focuses on effects from framing situations or messages in terms that acknowledge losses versus gains.

The goal of our first intervention was to increase the salience of information regarding the online renewal option that citizens saw in the subject line on the mailing envelope carrying the sticker renewal form (see Figure 1). We made two adjustments motivated by the knowledge that when some information is emphasized more than other information in a communication, the emphasized content will have greater impact on people's judgments.[18,19]

First, we embedded the black text of the subject line in a blue background to make it stand out on the exterior of an otherwise standard black-and-white

ServiceOntario pressure-sealed envelope (see reference 14).[20] Second, to increase the salience of benefits from online renewal, in the subject line on the envelope, we used the wording "Instant and easy renewal online" rather than "Renew online and receive a 10-day extension." Our reasoning was that not all consumers require a 10-day extension. Further, because renewing license plate stickers online might seem complex and daunting to people inexperienced with the procedure, focusing on its benefits could help ease people into trying an unfamiliar process (see Figure 2).

Research has shown that when people think about an immediate action, they often primarily focus on hassles or the mental effort required to perform the action instead of the benefits. For example, when deciding whether to adopt a new technology such as a smart watch, consumers are often predisposed to think first about the learning costs (time, for instance) associated with new tools.[21] Because of a well-documented process known as *output interference,* this can inhibit the consideration of potential benefits. In other words, the consideration of unwelcome factors interferes with the effective consideration of any subsequent factors.[22–24]

In light of these insights, we also changed the original messaging (see Figure 3) about the online renewal option printed on the back of the renewal form found inside the pressure-sealed envelope. Specifically, we designed our second and third interventions to emphasize in more detail the consumer benefits that accompany an online renewal. Our goal was to prompt

Figure 1. Standard messaging on the license plate sticker renewal envelope (control condition)

Figure 2. Salience messaging on the license plate sticker renewal envelope (treatment conditions 1, 2, and 3)

In the actual mailing sent out during the field experiment, the shaded area visible here was a pale blue, not gray.

consideration of the benefits before a person had time to think about any hassles or costs associated with undertaking an unfamiliar process. We framed the benefits of renewing online in two ways. In our second intervention, we directed people's attention to the gains or positives associated with the online renewal (see

Figure 4). In our third intervention, we applied one of the most robust findings in the behavioral science literature: that people are more averse to potential losses than they are attracted to equivalent potential gains (see research on loss aversion in, for example, reference 11).[25] Here we highlighted the negatives, particularly the time

Figure 3. Standard messaging on the back of the license plate sticker renewal form (control condition and treatment condition 1)

ServiceOntario

Left it to the last minute? No problem.
Vous avez attendu la dernière minute? Pas de problème.

Click. Print. Drive.
Print and carry your online receipt, valid for 10 days from your expiry date. It's proof you've renewed until your sticker arrives in the mail.

Visit us at
ServiceOntario.ca/PlateSticker

Cliquez. Imprimez. Prenez la route.
Imprimez votre reçu électronique et gardez-le sous la main. Il est valide pendant 10 jours à partir de la date d'expiration. C'est la preuve que vous avez renouvelé votre vignette en attendant de la recevoir par la poste

Visitez
ServiceOntario.ca/AutoCollant

ServiceOntario

Discover the convenience of <u>renewing online!</u>
Découvrez la convenance du renouvellement en ligne!

Why go online?
1. Save travel time
2. Save waiting time
3. Renew from the comfort of your home, 24/7
4. Easy and safe – just like online banking
5. Instant confirmation and legal proof of renewal

Pourquoi allez en ligne ?
1. Épargnez le temps de déplacement
2. Épargnez le délai d'attente
3. Remplacez du confort de votre maison, 24/7
4. Facile et sûr – comme banque en ligne
5. Confirmation instantanée et preuve légale de renouvellement

What are you waiting for? Visit us at
ServiceOntario.ca/RenewSticker

Qu'attendez-vous? Visitez
ServiceOntario.ca/Renouveler-la-Vignette

In this mailing, the words *renewing online!* and the website address were printed in red, in English and in French.

cost, of not choosing to renew online (see Figure 5). In addition, in both of these framing interventions on the back of the form we also used color to try to heighten the salience of parts of the gain and loss messages by printing some text in red instead of black. The colors used in our interventions are visible in our Supplemental Material published online.

Testing Our Interventions

In our study, 626,212 owners of registered vehicles in Ontario received one of four different versions of a sticker renewal letter over eight weeks from December 2013 to February 2014. In the control condition, owners received the provincial government's standard renewal letter (see Figures 1 and 3). The rest received envelopes with the color and text modifications described above (see Figure 2), as well as one of three different messages inside. What we call the *salience-only* condition (with the envelope altered but nothing else) featured the same message inside the envelope as the existing, standard renewal letter (see Figure 3). The *salience-gain* condition featured the gain-frame messaging and color

modifications inside the envelope emphasizing the gains of renewing online (see Figure 4). And the *salience-loss* condition featured the loss-frame messaging and color modifications inside the envelope stressing the cost of not renewing online (see Figure 5).

We manipulated which version of the renewal letter was mailed to vehicle owners each week, according to the schedule in Table 1. Ninety days before each vehicle owner's date of birth, when license plate stickers expire, ServiceOntario mails out renewal forms. As a consequence, vehicle owners' assignment to one of our four conditions depended on their license plate sticker expiration date. Although complete randomization of assignment to condition would have been ideal, system limitations involved with printing and tracking hundreds of thousands of renewal forms mandated this approach.

As can be seen in Table 1, each condition was run two times for one-week periods, with four weeks between the periods. Our primary measure of success (our dependent variable) was the percentage of vehicle owners who renewed online. We also measured the percentage of vehicle owners in our sample who renewed on time. As can be seen in

ServiceOntario

Don't miss out on the convenience of <u>renewing online</u>!
Découvrez la convenance du <u>renouvellement en ligne</u>!

Renewing in person:
1. Travel to ServiceOntario centre (20 minutes)
2. Wait in line (15 minutes)
3. Talk to agent (5 minutes)
4. Travel back to home/office (20 minutes)

Total estimated time: 1 hour or more

Renewing online:
Total estimated time: 10 minutes or less
in the convenience of your home, 24/7, instant,
easy and safe.

What are you waiting for? Visit us at
<u>ServiceOntario.ca/RenewOnline</u>

Renouvellement en personne:
1. Voyage pour entretenir le bureau d'Ontario (20 minutes)
2. Attente dans la ligne (15 minutes)
3. Entretien à l'agent (5 minutes)
4. Voyage de nouveau à la maison/au bureau (20 minutes)

Temps total: 1 heure ou plus

Renouvellement en ligne:
Temps total: 10 minutes ou moins
dans la commodité de votre maison, 24/7,
instant, facile et sûr.

Qu'attendez-vous? Visitez
<u>ServiceOntario.ca/Renouveler-en-Ligne</u>

In this mailing, the words *renewing online!*, the 10-minute time estimate, and the website address were printed in red, in English and in French.

Figure 6, each of our three treatment conditions increased online renewals in comparison to the standard letter. The salience-gain treatment condition achieved the largest relative increase of 42.7% (increasing from 10.3% to 14.7%).

A technical description of our statistical analysis can be found online in our Supplemental Material. To summarize, we used two statistical techniques to ascertain whether the differences in online and on-time renewal rates between groups of people who

Table 1. Design of mailing distribution for field experiment and weekly results

Letters mailed	Content	Treatment condition	Online renewals	On-time renewals
Block 1				
Week 1: 75,145	Standard messaging	Control	9.4%	71.9%
Week 2: 90,045	Modified envelope only	TC1: Salience only	11.7%	72.1%
Week 3: 75,797	Modified envelope and potential gain emphasized	TC2: Salience and gain	13.8%	74.0%
Week 4: 76,536	Modified envelope and potential loss emphasized	TC3: Salience and loss	13.0%	72.7%
Block 2				
Week 5: 76,923	Standard letter text	Control	11.2%	69.0%
Week 6: 84,897	Modified envelope only	TC1: Salience only	11.5%	76.5%
Week 7: 67,504	Modified envelope and potential gain emphasized	TC2: Salience and gain	15.5%	77.3%
Week 8: 78,900	Modified envelope and potential loss emphasized	TC3: Salience and loss	13.5%	74.5%

Note. TC1 = treatment condition 1; TC2 = treatment condition 2; TC3 = treatment condition 3.

Figure 6. Percentage of license plate stickers renewed online, averaged across two weeks for each treatment condition

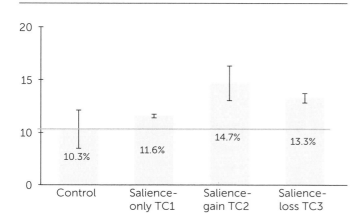

Error bars represent 95% confidence intervals based on eight weeks of observation. The bars display how much variation exists among data from each group. If two error bars overlap by less than a quarter of their total length (or do not overlap), the probability that the differences were observed by chance is less than 5% (that is, the statistical significance is $p < .05$). TC1 = treatment condition 1; TC2 = treatment condition 2; TC3 = treatment condition 3.

had received different renewal letters was greater than would be expected by chance. The more common and less stringent was *binomial logistic regression* (Models 1 and 2 in Supplemental Table 1 online). It showed that people who received any of the three experimental letters developed for this trial were statistically more likely to renew their license plate stickers online and on time. Moreover, using this technique, we also found that both the salience-gain and salience-loss letters performed significantly better than the salience-only letter in terms of spurring online and on-time renewals. These results suggest that increasing the salience of the online service and emphasizing its relative gains helped encourage more consumers to take advantage of the online service.

The more stringent technique, called *multilevel binomial logistic regression* (Models 3 and 4 in Supplemental Table 1 online), is similar but was used to take into account a potential flaw in our trial design. Randomized controlled trials (RCTs) are normally conducted using random number generators or some other means of ensuring that each participant has an equal chance of receiving one of the various treatments (in this case, letters). In our trial, however, it was only possible to alter the version of the letter that was sent on a weekly

basis. This created a potential problem, in that participants receiving a particular letter might exhibit behavior similar to the behavior of others receiving that same letter not because of the content of that letter but because of other coincident events occurring that week (for example, a weather event keeping people indoors and out of government offices). Because such factors could result in statistical errors, we created multilevel models to account for them. The results of these models suggest that only the salience-gain and salience-loss letters had significant positive effects on online renewals and that only the salience-gain letter had any effect on on-time renewals. This more stringent statistical analysis thus gives us greater confidence that the salience-gain letter prompted the best response of the four letters and that its apparent effect on online renewals is not due to chance.

The increased use of the online renewal service during our eight-week experimental period saved the government approximately $28,000 in transaction fees by reducing the number of in-person transactions in ServiceOntario centers, which are paid according to the number of in-person transactions processed. This estimate also takes into account marginal costs for the online service associated with meeting an increase in demand of this magnitude. We project that if the best-performing salience-gain treatment condition is adopted permanently in Ontario, approximately $612,000 would be saved annually, and this gain would be achieved at virtually zero cost to the government.

We also observed suggestive evidence that one of our interventions designed to increase online renewal service use also increased the number of on-time license plate sticker renewals. Such an additional benefit from increasing usage of an online service could be expected on the basis that online services are more convenient, are available at all times, and therefore pose fewer barriers that may encourage procrastination. However, as none of our interventions specifically addressed timely renewals, any effect on timely renewals would presumably be mediated through an increase in online renewals. Thus our evidence of this effect is less robust.

Figure 7 displays the on-time renewal rates by type of letter (for weekly results, see Table 1). Compared with the control condition, the salience-gain condition led to a 7.5% relative increase (from 70.4% to 75.7%) in timely renewals. The bottom half of Supplemental

Figure 7. Percentage of license plate stickers renewed on time, averaged across two weeks for each treatment condition

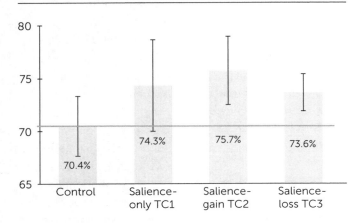

Error bars represent 95% confidence intervals based on eight weeks of observation. The bars display how much variation exists among data from each group. If two error bars overlap by less than a quarter of their total length (or do not overlap), the probability that the differences were observed by chance is less than 5% (that is, the statistical significance is $p < .05$). TC1 = treatment condition 1; TC2 = treatment condition 2; TC3 = treatment condition 3.

Table 1 online presents both the simple binary logistic regression results (Models 1 and 2) as well as the multilevel binary logistic regression results (Models 3 and 4). Both types of analyses agree on one observation: The salience-gain condition was most effective. In addition, the 1.3 times larger odds of on-time renewal in the salience-gain condition compared with the control condition can be considered a significant trend (highly significant according to the simple binary logistic regression and marginally significant according to the multilevel logistic regression). At minimum, we can conclude that our gain-frame messaging intervention on the back of the renewal form also had a significant, positive impact on timely renewals.

Subtle, Low-Cost Changes Have Impact

In a large-scale RCT in which people made real, consequential decisions, we observed that even subtle changes in messaging that apply behavioral principles can substantially influence people's actions. It is important to note here that our interventions did not introduce citizens to the online service for the first time. The standard letter already directed vehicle owners to

the ServiceOntario online renewal service and displayed its Internet address. Instead, the intervention increased participation in an existing government program, a benefit to both citizens and public policy due to its increased convenience and lower cost.

Our results add to the growing number of demonstrations of how simple and often cost-free interventions rooted in behavioral science research can be applied to help people make better decisions, without resorting to financial incentives or restricting freedom of choice. The interventions we tested, consistent with research on choice architecture and nudging (see reference 8),[26] could be easily translated to other public policy realms. Highlighting communications materials to increase the salience of key messages and testing various gain and loss frames may be useful in helping citizens take advantage of any number of public services and benefits, such as the various government borrowing and savings programs that have seen improved participation due to interventions designed by the White House's Social and Behavioral Sciences Team (SBST).[27]

Our results also reinforces the finding that using RCTs in the field is a feasible and valuable tool for testing some potential policy interventions.[28] Staging such research allows for potent, rigorous comparison of multiple candidate interventions to determine which is the most effective in real-world contexts. Also, it can be implemented at very low cost when the proposed interventions are simply variants of existing processes, as was the case with our research.

It is also noteworthy that our findings are not consistent with the well-established finding that avoiding losses is a particularly strong motivator (see reference 11 and reference 25). Our messaging that emphasized potential gains (the gain frame) on the back of the renewal form was most effective and, in particular, more effective than the messaging that emphasized potential losses (the loss frame). This could be because people are already anticipating losses in the form of expected hassles when they consider using the in-person service instead of the online technology (see reference 21). That possibility may undermine effects from any additional loss thoughts. This unexpected finding illustrates the importance of testing even very fundamental assumptions before implementing a policy.

Our ability to explain this divergence from what has been observed in the loss aversion literature is limited by several imposed methodological constraints. That includes limitations regarding the number of conditions that we could run in an eight-week experimental period and the randomization capabilities of the ServiceOntario's printer. For example, our salience-gain and salience-loss treatment conditions varied in several ways in addition to the framing. In particular, the salience-loss condition focused primarily on time savings and losses and presented both the negatives of not renewing online and the positives of renewing online. It did this in a particular order: It mentioned the negatives first, then the positives (see, for example, query theory; see reference 24). The salience-gain condition, on the other hand, focused only on the positives of renewing online, with no particular focus on time savings and losses. In addition, the salience-loss condition was much more specific when naming costs and benefits in that it mentioned very specific times, such as "wait in line (15 minutes)," in comparison to the benefits mentioned in the salience-gain condition ("save waiting time").

Such differences make it difficult to tease apart the respective influences of each condition. Perhaps our findings reinforce the observation that a frame focused on loss is simply not effective when the focal attribute is time. That may be because people typically don't view time investments as costs.[29] Follow-up research could manipulate these elements in a more controlled manner to better understand their contribution. Exploring this and other potential mechanisms of our findings in laboratory studies could help refine and improve our interventions.

It is also worth noting that despite the success of our interventions relative to the status quo, the absolute number of citizens who used online renewal services was low—only 14.7% in the most effective condition. At this point, we can only speculate as to why. It is possible that many citizens did not read the content we added to the envelope or the renewal form with sufficient attention to encounter the online renewal opportunity. As a result, citizens may have habitually continued with the in-person service.

Another possibility is that some people are uncomfortable with conducting online transactions requiring personal information because of security and privacy concerns.[30] This may particularly be true for older adults who are less familiar with such processes.[31] Given that 84% of Ontarians have expressed interest in accessing government services online (see reference 2) but only 14.7% did so after our most successful intervention, we conclude that enormous potential continues to exist for behavioral science–based interventions to further narrow this intention–action gap.

Our experimental design, necessitated by practical constraints, introduced the possibility that our results could alternatively be explained by some other phenomenon that produced a four-week trend in online renewals, which was subsequently repeated the following four weeks. Although we see this alternative explanation as unlikely, it is impossible to rule out. It further illustrates the trade-offs between experimental control and the real-world field studies required to achieve external validity. In light of our positive results, however, ServiceOntario has embraced our most successful approach to nudge the people it serves to take advantage of its online renewal service. At the end of February 2015, it implemented the features of our salience-gain test condition by changing its standard mailing to all customers. The agency added the blue color and the text changes to the envelope and replaced the standard message about the online renewal option on the back of the renewal form with the positive gain-frame messaging and red color modification.

Aggregate online renewal rates every month after this province-wide implementation enabled us to compare year-over-year increases in online renewals for the seven months immediately before and after the implementation of the salience-gain letter. As can be seen in the dashed black line of Figure 8, after the salience-gain letter was implemented province-wide, there is a more pronounced increase in the percentage of license plate stickers renewed online each month compared with the same month in the previous year (represented by the solid gray line). To assess whether this increase is statistically significant, we conducted a mixed-method analysis of variance to control for any seasonal effects during the months in which the salience-gain letter was first implemented. An in-depth description of the statistical analysis and results can be found online in our Supplemental Material. To summarize, this analysis revealed a significant positive interaction, indicating that in the months after the salience-gain letter was implemented in Ontario, the year-over-year increases in the use of online services accelerated significantly, by about 1%.

Figure 8. Percentage of license plate stickers renewed online over time, before and after implementation of the salience-gain treatment

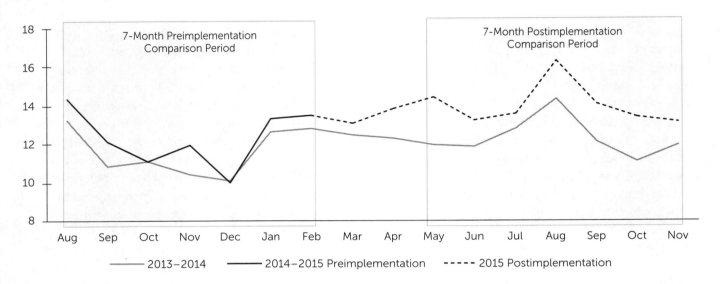

The two gray-shaded boxes highlight the periods used to calculate the means in the interaction shown in Figure 4 in the online Supplemental Material.

Managerial Takeaways

In addition to our findings, we are sharing some reflections on the process we used to obtain these results. Our research is part of an ongoing collaboration between the Government of Ontario's BIU and the Rotman School of Management's BEAR to improve savings, efficiency, and well-being in Ontario. Through this collaboration, we've learned several practical lessons that may be of use to others working to apply behavioral science insights in the public policy realm:

- Whenever possible, a fully randomized experimental design is preferable. If this is not an option, it is crucial to come up with a design that limits the influence of confounds to ensure that measured effects are caused by the interventions.
- Data requirements for a study must be communicated clearly to all relevant parties. Further, data collection should be pretested before an RCT is conducted to ensure that all data are captured.
- A thorough application of behavioral insights with RCTs requires a research team with strong policy

and program knowledge, an understanding of government, and support from academics with both theoretical and experimental expertise.
- Collaborations between scholars and government employees benefit from a division of labor that takes advantage of their respective expertise. These groups need strong administrative support.
- Researchers need allies to explore the promise of behavioral insights to improve public policy. Organized outreach, education, and support from senior leadership, and early adopters are all needed.
- A behavioral insights–driven philosophy can help a government better understand the people it serves.
- Outcomes that benefit citizens can lead to better outcomes for government programs.

This project has strengthened our confidence that applying behavioral insights and principles can produce measurable and positive outcomes at low cost. It has also reinforced our belief that collaborations such as the one described above can improve the performance of existing government programs.

author affiliation

Castelo, Columbia Business School, Columbia University; Hardy, Central Innovation Hub, Government of Canada; House, Behavioural Insights Unit (BIU), Government of Ontario, and Behavioural Economics in Action research hub (BEAR) at Rotman School of Management, University of Toronto; Mazar, BEAR, Rotman School of Management, University of Toronto, and Global INsights Initiative (GINI), World Bank; and Tsai and Zhao, BEAR, Rotman School of Management, University of Toronto. Corresponding authors' e-mail addresses: elizabeth.hardy@pco-bcp.gc.ca and nina@ninamazar.com.

author note

The authors are listed in alphabetical order. Julian House was responsible for the data analysis and interpretation; Nina Mazar was the research project lead. The research was conducted while Elizabeth Hardy was a manager in the Behavioural Insights Unit of the Government of Ontario (from 2013 to 2015). The research was supported by a TD Bank Group Research Fund awarded to BEAR.

supplemental material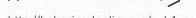

- http://behavioralpolicy.org/vol-1-no-2/mazar
- Methods & Analysis
- Additional Reference

References

1. Enright, A. (2015). *U.S. annual e-retail sales surpass $300 billion for the first time*. Retrieved from Internet Retailer website: https://www.internetretailer.com/2015/02/17/us-annual-e-retail-sales-surpass-300-billion-first-ti
2. Jordan, M., Belmonte, D., Fowell, L. H., Tanaka, D., & Wagner, J. (2012). *Next generation of eservices: Enhancing service delivery in the Canadian public sector*. Retrieved from PwC website: http://www.pwc.com/en_GX/gx/psrc/pdf/citizen-compass.pdf
3. Soman, D. (2015). *The last mile: Creating social and economic value from behavioral insights*. Toronto, Ontario, Canada: University of Toronto Press.
4. Thaler, R., & Benartzi, S. (2004). Save More Tomorrow™: Using behavioral economics to increase employee saving. *Journal of Political Economy, 112*(Suppl. S1), S164–S187.
5. Bendapudi, N., Singh, S. N., & Bendapudi, V. (1996). Enhancing helping behavior: An integrative framework for promotion planning. *Journal of Marketing, 60*(3), 33–49.
6. House of Lords. (2011). *Behavior change report*. Retrieved from http://www.parliament.uk/business/committees/committees-a-z/lords-select/science-and-technology-committee/news/behaviour-change-published

7. Ly, K., & Soman, D. (2013). *Nudging around the world*. Retrieved from University of Toronto, Rotman School of Management website: http://cd-www.rotman.utoronto.ca/-/media/Files/Programs-and-Areas/behavioural-economics/Nudging%20Around%20The%20World_Sep2013.pdf
8. Thaler, R., & Sunstein, C. (2008). *Nudge: Improving decisions about health, wealth, and happiness*. New Haven, CT: Yale University Press.
9. Dinner, I., Johnson, E. J., Goldstein, D. G., & Liu, K. (2011). Partitioning default effects: Why people choose not to choose. *Journal of Experimental Psychology: Applied, 17*, 332–341.
10. Kahneman, D., Knetsch, J. L., & Thaler, R. H. (1990). Experimental tests of the endowment effect and the Coase theorem. *Journal of Political Economy, 98*, 1325–1348. http://doi.org/10.1086/261737
11. Kahneman, D., Knetsch, J. L., & Thaler, R. H. (1991). Anomalies: The endowment effect, loss aversion, and status quo bias. *Journal of Economic Perspectives, 5*(1), 193–206. http://doi.org/10.1257/jep.5.1.193
12. Johnson, E. J., & Goldstein, D. (2003, November 21). Do defaults save lives? *Science, 302*, 1338–1339. http://doi.org/10.1126/science.1091721
13. Madrian, B. C., & Shea, D. F. (2001). The power of suggestion: Inertia in 401(k) participation and savings behavior. *The Quarterly Journal of Economics, 116*, 1149–1187.
14. UK Cabinet Office Behavioural Insights Team. (2012). *Applying behavioural insights to reduce fraud, error and debt*. Retrieved from https://www.gov.uk/government/uploads/system/uploads/attachment_data/file/%20%2060539/BIT_FraudErrorDebt_accessible.pdf
15. Hallsworth, M., List, J., Metcalfe, R., & Vlaev, I. (2014). *The behavioralist as tax collector: Using natural field experiments to enhance tax compliance* (NBER Working Paper 20007). Retrieved from National Bureau of Economic Research website: http://www.nber.org/papers/w20007
16. Shu, L. L., Mazar, N., Gino, F., Ariely, D., & Bazerman, M. H. (2012). Signing at the beginning makes ethics salient and decreases dishonest self-reports in comparison to signing at the end. *Proceedings of the National Academy of Sciences, USA, 109*, 15197–15200. http://doi.org/10.1073/pnas.1209746109
17. Zhao, M., Lee, L., & Soman, D. (2012). Crossing the virtual boundary: The effect of task-irrelevant environmental cues on task implementation. *Psychological Science, 23*, 1200–1207. http://doi.org/10.1177/0956797612441608
18. Alba, J. W., & Chattopadhyay, A. (1986). Salience effects in brand recall. *Journal of Marketing Research, 23*, 363–369.
19. Taylor, S. E., & Thompson, S. C. (1982). Stalking the elusive "vividness" effect. *Psychological Review, 89*, 155–181.
20. Kahneman, D. (2011). *Thinking, fast and slow*. New York, NY: Farrar, Straus and Giroux.
21. Zhao, M., Hoeffler, S., & Zauberman, G. (2007). Mental simulation and preference consistency over time: The role of process- versus outcome-focused thoughts. *Journal of Marketing Research, 44*, 379–388.
22. Anderson, M. C., & Neely, J. H. (1996). Interference and inhibition in memory retrieval. In E. Bjork & R. Bjork (Eds.), *Memory handbook of perception and cognition* (pp. 237–313). San Diego, CA: Academic Press.
23. Hoch, S. J. (1984). Availability and interference in predictive judgment. *Journal of Experimental Psychology: Learning, Memory, and Cognition, 10*, 649–662.
24. Johnson, E. J., Häubl, G., & Keinan, A. (2007). Aspects of endowment: A query theory of value construction. *Journal of Experimental Psychology: Learning, Memory, and Cognition, 33*, 461–474. http://doi.org/10.1037/0278-7393.33.3.461

25. Kahneman, D., & Tversky, A. (1979). Prospect theory: An analysis of decision under risk. *Econometrica, 47,* 263–292.

26. Johnson, E. J., Shu, S. B., Dellaert, B. G. C., Fox, C., Goldstein, D. G., Häubl, G., . . . Weber, E. U. (2012). Beyond nudges: Tools of a choice architecture. *Marketing Letters, 23,* 487–504. http://doi.org/10.1007/s11002-012-9186-1

27. Social and Behavioral Sciences Team. (2015). *Annual report.* Retrieved from White House website: https://www.whitehouse.gov/sites/default/files/microsites/ostp/sbst_2015_annual_report_final_9_14_15.pdf

28. Haynes, L., Service, O., Goldacre, B., & Torgerson, D. (2012). *Test, learn, adapt: Developing public policy with randomised controlled trials.* Retrieved from United Kingdom Cabinet Office website: https://www.gov.uk/government/uploads/system/uploads/attachment_data/file/62529/TLA-1906126.pdf

29. Leclerc, F., Schmitt, B. H., & Dubé, L. (1995). Waiting time and decision making: Is time like money? *Journal of Consumer Research, 22,* 110–119.

30. Carter, L., & Bélanger, F. (2005). The utilization of e-government services: Citizen trust, innovation and acceptance factors. *Information Systems Journal, 15,* 5–25.

31. Forsythe, S. M., & Shi, B. (2003). Consumer patronage and risk perceptions in Internet shopping. *Journal of Business Research, 56,* 867–875.

Blinding prosecutors to defendants' race: A policy proposal to reduce unconscious bias in the criminal justice system

Sunita Sah, Christopher T. Robertson, & Shima B. Baughman

Summary. Racial minorities are disproportionately imprisoned in the United States. This disparity is unlikely to be due solely to differences in criminal behavior. Behavioral science research has documented that prosecutors harbor unconscious racial biases. These unconscious biases play a role whenever prosecutors exercise their broad discretion, such as in choosing what crimes to charge and when negotiating plea bargains. To reduce this risk of unconscious racial bias, we propose a policy change: Prosecutors should be blinded to the race of criminal defendants wherever feasible. This could be accomplished by removing information identifying or suggesting the defendant's race from police dossiers shared with prosecutors and by avoiding mentions of race in conversations between prosecutors and defense attorneys. Race is almost always irrelevant to the merits of a criminal prosecution; it should be omitted from the proceedings whenever possible for the sake of justice.

Prosecutors may have more independent power and discretion than any other government officials in the United States.[1] Prosecutors decide whether to initiate criminal proceedings, what charges to file or bring before a grand jury, how and when to prosecute individuals, and what penalties to seek. For a given criminal behavior, half a dozen charges might apply, ranging from minor misdemeanors to the most serious felonies. A prosecutor can decline to press charges altogether or stack charges by characterizing the same behavior as

Sah, S., Robertson, C. T., & Baughman, S. B. (2015). Blinding prosecutors to defendants' race: A policy proposal to reduce unconscious bias in the criminal justice system. *Behavioral Science & Policy, 1*(2).

violating the law dozens of times (charging each phone call made as part of a drug transaction as a crime, for instance). Once charged, about 95% of criminal cases are resolved through plea bargaining, where prosecutors can defer prosecution, suspend a sentence, minimize factual allegations in ways that virtually guarantee a light sentence, or insist on the most severe penalties.[2] If a case does go to trial, a prosecutor's sentencing demand provides an influential reference point (an anchor) for a defense attorney's response in plea negotiations and the judge's final sentencing decision.[3]

Prosecutors typically do not need to articulate the bases for their discretionary decisions,[4,5] and these decisions receive only minimal scrutiny from the courts.

Although the U.S. Constitution theoretically limits the discretion of prosecutors (to target a particular race prejudicially, for instance), such protections are exceedingly difficult to invoke,[6] especially if a prosecutor's unconscious rather than intentional bias is in play.[7] This context prompts us to offer an important and novel proposal with the potential to help make the justice system blind to race.

Prosecutors, we believe, should be unaware of defendants' race whenever possible. Implementing such a significant change would be challenging, clearly. But evidence of persistent disparities regarding the proportion of racial minorities that are put in prison makes the need for change apparent. And growing evidence that prosecutors' unconscious biases contribute to that imbalance gives us a potentially powerful target for efforts to produce positive and vitally needed change.

Racial Bias in the Criminal Justice System

In 2010 in the United States, Blacks made up 38% of all prisoners, although they made up only 12% of the national population.[8] That same year, about one in 23 Black men was in prison, compared with one in 147 White men.[9] The causes of this racial disparity are many and complex. Socioeconomic factors (poverty and lower educational achievement, for example) play a role. So may inequitable police behavior that, for example, leads to Blacks being stopped and frisked more often than Whites are.[10,11]

Black defendants also tend to receive harsher sentences than White defendants do, even when both the severity of the crime and previous criminal history are taken into account.[12] For example, harsher punishment was applied to crimes related to crack cocaine versus powder cocaine in federal sentencing guidelines, which tended to punish Blacks more harshly because they were more likely to be arrested with crack cocaine than powder cocaine. To minimize this disparate impact on Blacks, Congress passed the Fair Sentencing Act in 2010, which reduced the unequal penalties and eliminated the five-year mandatory minimum sentence for simple crack cocaine possession. This new law addressed the racial bias perpetrated by the old regime that led to low-level crack dealers, who were often Black, receiving more severe sentences than wholesale suppliers of powdered cocaine.[13]

One important cause of the racial discrepancy among prisoners, however, is bias that affects discretionary decisions made by prosecutors.[14–17] A recent review of empirical studies examining prosecutorial decision making and race found that most of the studies suggested that the defendants' "race directly or indirectly influenced case outcomes, even when a host of other legal or extra-legal factors are taken into account."[17] Minorities, particularly Black males, "receive disproportionately harsher treatment at each stage of the prosecutorial decision-making process."[18] Indeed, prosecutors in predominantly Black communities have been shown to make racially biased decisions, such as overcharging Black youth,[19] which, in turn, perpetuates racial stereotypes.[20,21] Further, Black children in the United States are much more likely than White children to be sentenced as adults,[22] probably because Black juveniles are perceived to be older and less childlike than White juveniles.[23,24]

These data do not suggest that prosecutors are overtly racist, although some may be. Instead, research documents that bias can infect even people with the best of intentions, including physicians and other professionals.[25,26] Prosecutors are humans with bounded rationality, making decisions in a cultural milieu that shapes their perceptions and decisions on an unconscious level.[15,27,28] Generally, bias increases in ambiguous situations,[20,29–33] and as we described previously, decisions on what and how many charges to file against a defendant are inherently ambiguous.

Behavioral science researchers have demonstrated that people unknowingly misremember case facts in racially biased ways.[34,35] For example, there is a greater tendency to remember aggressive actions (e.g., punches or kicks) if a suspect is Black.[34] In fact, it appears that the more stereotypically Black a defendant is perceived to be, the more likely that person is to be sentenced to death.[36] In one study, Stanford University students viewed photographs of Black men, rating each one on the degree to which the person's appearance was stereotypically Black. The students were told they could base their decisions on any of the features of the photographed subjects to make their decisions, including noses, lips, skin tone, and hair. Unbeknownst to the students, each man in the images had been convicted of murdering a White person. The men the students rated as appearing more stereotypically Black were more likely to have been sentenced to death in criminal proceedings.[36] Other research has demonstrated that lighter skin tones may lead to more lenient judgments and prison sentences.[20,37]

Although bias exists throughout the criminal justice system, bias in prosecutorial decisions has a potentially disproportionate impact, given that most criminal cases do not go to trial and prosecutors exercise such wide discretion in handling them. One might hope that selecting prosecutors of good faith and asking them to behave professionally could avert racial bias. In this vein, in 2014, the Department of Justice reaffirmed its policy that "in making decisions . . . law enforcement officers may not use race."[38] Such a policy, although laudable, unfortunately cannot prevent unconscious bias.

Prosecutorial decisions are made in a more deliberative fashion than, for example, split-second decisions made by police to shoot or not shoot. However, even with deliberative decisions, the ability to self-regulate bias is difficult: Moral reasoning is usually a post hoc construction, generated after a (usually intuitive) judgment has been reached,[39] often influenced by erroneous factors.[40] People exhibiting bias are typically unaware that they are doing so, and bias is often unintentional.[33,41,42] Educating people on unconscious bias often leads them to be convinced that other people are biased but that they themselves are not.[29] Accordingly, strategies to encourage people to become less biased are usually not sufficient.

One program that had some success in reducing racial disparities was the 2006 Prosecution and Racial Justice Program of the Vera Institute of Justice. Prosecutors collected and published data on defendant and victim race for each offense category and the prosecutorial action taken at each stage of criminal proceedings.[43] These data exposed that similarly situated defendants of different races were treated differently at each stage of discretion: initial case screening, charging, plea offers, and final disposition. For instance, in Wisconsin, the data showed that prosecutors were charging Black defendants at higher rates than White defendants for drug possession. With this information, the district attorney made an office policy to refer suspects to drug treatment rather than charging them in an attempt to reduce racial bias in charging. However, this approach requires a large investment from overburdened prosecutorial offices to collect and analyze their data to reveal trends in racial disparity. It also requires that individual prosecutors be motivated to

consciously avoid bias or at least be motivated to appear unbiased.[44,45] This motivation is often led by societal norms or public pressure regarding racial attitudes and inequality, which varies by jurisdiction. There presently is no complete solution to eliminate racial bias in prosecutorial decisions.

Blinding: An Alternative Approach to Managing Bias

An alternative way to manage bias is to acknowledge its existence and create institutional procedures to prevent bias from influencing important decisions. The psychologist Robert Rosenthal, a leading methodologist, concluded that the best way to reduce the chances of bias unconsciously affecting decision processes is to keep the process "as blind as possible for as long as possible."[46]

Blinding (or *masking*) to improve decisionmaking has a long history in different domains. For example, having musicians audition behind a screen decreased gender bias and increased the acceptance rate of women into symphony orchestras.[47] In medical science, both subjects and researchers are, whenever feasible, kept unaware of who is in the treatment or control groups of clinical trials, in an effort to achieve unbiased results.[48] Meta-analyses have shown that such blinding reduces the number of false positives in science experiments.[49,50] Similarly, editors of scholarly journals routinely remove authors' names and institutions from submissions so they can assess articles on their scientific merits alone.[51] Likewise, to avoid possible favoritism, some professors mask students' identities on papers when grading.[52]

Blinding is already in use in other stages of the criminal justice process. For example, lineups are widely acknowledged to be best conducted by an officer who does not know which person is the suspect, so as not to pollute the eyewitness's perceptions.[53,54] This practice of blind administration of lineups was originally highly controversial. Iowa State University professor Gary Wells first proposed implementing blinding of police to suspect lineups in 1988,[55] although evidence of bias and erroneous identification had been accumulating for years before that. More than a decade later, in 1999, the U.S. Department of Justice published a set of best practices for conducting police lineups[56] that excluded blind procedures (although it acknowledged that having investigators who did not know which person in the lineup was the suspect was desirable) because blinding "may be impractical for some jurisdictions to implement" (p. 9).[56] Nevertheless, individual jurisdictions experimented with blind procedures.[57] By 2014, the National Research Council recommended unreservedly that all lineups should be conducted with the benefits of blinding.[58]

Blinding has also been recommended for forensic scientists and other expert witnesses, so that attorneys for either side in a case do not influence and undermine their scientific expertise.[32] More generally, the rules of evidence (which determine what is permissible in court) can be understood as an elaborate blinding procedure, designed to ensure that juries are not exposed to irrelevant or unreliable evidence, recognizing that for the purpose of assessing guilt, some factors are more prejudicial than probative.[59]

The Case for Blinded Prosecutors

The success of the long-standing practice of blinding in other contexts gives credence to our proposal that prosecutors should be blinded to the race of criminal defendants whenever possible. Prosecutors, like other professionals, cannot be biased by what they do not know. In addition to mitigating unconscious bias, the blinding of prosecutors also mitigates any conscious racism, which may infect some prosecutors.

Federal prosecutors already use a race-blinding procedure for death penalty decisions. The Department of Justice requires that attorneys on committees of capital cases (which determine death eligibility) review each defendant file only after information related to the race of the defendant has been removed.[60] Only paralegal assistants who collect statistics know the defendants' races. The question is how far this practice can and should be expanded. We believe there is potential for broader use of race blinding by other prosecutors. Prosecutors are a good target for race blinding given their substantial power and impact, particularly with two pivotal decisions: the filing of charges and the negotiation of plea bargains.

Charging Decisions

Prosecutorial practice varies in different jurisdictions. For petty offenses, a prosecutor may make key decisions in

court while facing defendants, making blinding infeasible (unless that dynamic itself is reformed). In many jurisdictions, however, prosecutors do not see defendants in person when making initial charging decisions; these are based on information provided in police dossiers, in which race could be redacted. In fact, the trend is for such information to be conveyed to prosecutors electronically, making it easier to filter the race information, perhaps automatically by electronic tools or by intermediaries. In either case, race information could be retained for other uses such as identification or demographic tracking. As the Department of Justice capital-case review committees show, some assistants can have access to a full criminal file while decision-makers see only race-blind information.

Plea Bargaining

Although defendants retain the ultimate choice about whether to accept any deal, the prosecuting and defense attorneys actually negotiate that deal, and the prosecutor need not be exposed to the race of the defendant. In some jurisdictions, plea bargaining happens at arraignments with defendants in the same room. But this practice is neither uniform nor necessary. Thus, the two steps that are conclusive for the vast majority of cases—charging decisions and plea bargaining—can potentially be blinded to race.

Limitations, Challenges, and the Need for Pilot Testing

Although we argue for the value of race blinding procedures, we acknowledge that there will be difficulties and limitations in implementing such a policy. Race should have no legitimate role in the vast majority of charging decisions. However, in rare situations, such as prosecutions for hate crime, the race of an alleged perpetrator is relevant. In these cases, the necessary information can be provided to prosecutors.

For cases in which race is irrelevant, the blinding strategy will be effective at eliminating bias only to the extent that prosecutors are unable to infer race from other information available to them. Thus, it will be necessary to remove information that could reveal race, such as photos of a defendant; the defendant's name;[61] and, in racially segregated communities, the defendant's address. The practicalities of removing all race-related information could become complex. Further, race blinding may not be feasible if photos contain relevant information (such as defensive wounds on the defendant's skin) or eyewitness testimony describes a perpetrator's race.

To prevent prosecutors from inferring race from the defendants' names, court documents could instead identify defendants with assigned numbers (such as driver's license numbers). That said, removing names may have other unintended effects, such as reducing empathy, leading to harsher decisions toward anonymous defendants.[62] An alternative approach would be the use of random race-neutral pseudonyms to achieve anonymity without erasing all trace that a person is involved.

The severity of punishment is a question for the legislature. If race blinding succeeds, it levels the playing field for all by promoting equality, even if it decreases bias favorable to White defendants (often referred to as *White privilege*).[63-65] Both unjustified leniency for Whites and unjustified harsher punishments for Blacks were revealed in 2015 by the U.S. Department of Justice Civil Rights Division's investigation of the Ferguson (Missouri) Police Department. Of the many examples discussed in the report, one clearly highlighted the double standards: Whites were more likely to have citations, fines, and fees eliminated by city officials, whereas Blacks were punished for the same minor transgressions with expensive tickets and judgments punishing their perceived lack of personal responsibility (pp. 74–75).[66] That said, in other contexts, punishments may be harsher for Whites than for Blacks.[17] Blinding may create racial equity for both Black and White defendants.

Given that race blinding may not be feasible in some situations, may fail, or may have unintended consequences, the best path forward is to pilot-test this intervention and gauge its effectiveness. Pilot testing would allow researchers to uncover (and perhaps creatively address) challenges in the practical implementation of race blinding; evaluate on a smaller scale the precise impact, success, and value of race blinding; and expose any potential unintended consequences.[33,67-69] Sequential rollouts in different jurisdictions are also valuable, as they allow for continued monitoring and assessment in varying contexts.

In theory, prosecutors could be blinded to other information that may activate biases, including the race of the victim or the gender of the defendant or victim. These reforms should be considered on their own merits, including whether empirical evidence demonstrates that these variables are biasing prosecutorial decisions in a systematic fashion that is irrelevant to the proper application of the law. These considerations would also apply to whether blinding could be expanded to other decision-makers, including defense attorneys, judges, juries, and parole boards.

Impact and Cost Effectiveness

The need to eliminate race bias in prosecution is urgent. Racial biases can substantially distort decisions,[61,70] and prosecutorial bias alone leads to a substantial increase in the duration and severity of punishment for minorities. A study using 222,542 cases in New York County during 2010–2011 found that Black defendants were 10% more likely to be detained pretrial compared with White defendants charged with similar crimes, and they were 13% more likely to receive offers of prison sentences during plea bargaining.[71] Given that a prosecutor typically handles dozens of felonies and over a hundred misdemeanors per year,[72] the impact of racial bias is compounded. Approximately 27,000 state prosecutors deal with 2.9 million felony cases per year, and 6,075 federal prosecutors secure 82,000 convictions per year, not to mention the millions of prosecutorial decisions that are made on misdemeanor charges.[73,74] Two-thirds of those convicted of a felony go to prison, and the average sentence is about five years,[75] at a cost of $25,000 per prisoner per year.[76] Therefore, given that prosecutors are responsible for hundreds of person-years of incarceration annually and thus millions of dollars of public money, even a marginal reduction in bias may have a substantial effect.

These numbers have an impact that extends beyond the direct experiences of people sentenced to do time. As The Pew Charitable Trusts reported in 2010, the income of households and the educational success of children in those households decline when parents are put in jail.[77] The tangible and intangible costs to the prisoners, their families, and the broader society are tremendous.

Successfully blinding prosecutors to defendants' race may also improve the perceived legitimacy of prosecutorial decisions, which may enhance compliance with the law.[78] As important as anything else, it would advance some of the fundamental goals of our government: the equal treatment of all citizens and justice for all.

A New Standard: Blinding Prosecutors to Defendants' Race

If race blinding proves to be effective after pilot testing, we recommend that local and state prosecutors and the federal Department of Justice adopt race blinding as a uniform practice. We recommend that national and statewide associations of prosecutors (for example, the National District Attorneys Association), as well as broader organizations such as the American Bar Association (ABA), support implementation of the reforms. Furthermore, we recommend that this imperative be written into ethical codes and guidelines, such as the U.S. Attorneys' Handbook Chapter 9-27.000 (USAM) and Rule 3.8 of the ABA Model Rules of Professional Conduct (1983). Our reform also relies on the ethical behavior of attorneys, police, and other intermediaries who would not leak the race of the defendant to prosecutors. Adoption of this norm into the current ethical code could build on the current norms of confidentiality.

Race disparities pervade criminal justice decision-making in America. Among criminal-justice actors, the decisions of prosecutors are the least reviewable, are exercised with the most discretion, and are impactful. Blinding has been used as a tool to reduce gender and race discrimination in many fields, and its value is grounded in empirical evidence. We believe that blinding prosecutors to a defendant's race wherever feasible is a timely and important proposal.

We acknowledge that there will be practical implementation challenges and risks. Our primary aim with this proposal is to instigate a discussion on the merits and drawbacks of blinding prosecutors to race and to encourage pilot tests. The Department of Justice demonstrated the feasibility of race blinding for federal prosecutors[60] and state prosecutors could follow suit with similar procedures for their own death penalty cases. Expanding race blinding to other prosecutorial decisions may seem impractical; but, if the history of blind police lineups is any guide,[55] the jurisdictions most committed to racial equality and behaviorally informed policymaking will prove otherwise.

author affiliation

Sah, Johnson Graduate School of Management, Cornell University; Robertson, College of Law, University of Arizona; Baughman, College of Law, University of Utah. Corresponding author's e-mail: sunita.sah@cornell.edu

References

1. Bibas, S. (2009). Prosecutorial regulation versus prosecutorial accountability. *University of Pennsylvania Law Review, 157,* 959–1016.
2. Bibas, S. (2006). Transparency and participation in criminal procedure. *New York University Law Review, 86,* 911–912.
3. Englich, B. (2006). Blind or biased? Justitia's susceptibility to anchoring effects in the courtroom based on given numerical representations. *Law & Policy, 28,* 497–514.
4. Rabin, R. L. (1972). Agency criminal referrals in the federal system: An empirical study of prosecutorial discretion. *Stanford Law Review, 24,* 1036–1091.
5. Leonetti, C. (2012). When the emperor has no clothes III: Personnel policies and conflicts of interest in prosecutors' offices. *Cornell Journal of Law and Public Policy, 22,* 53–92.
6. Wayte v. United States, 470 U.S. 598 (1985).
7. McCleskey v. Kemp, 481 U.S. 279 (1987).
8. Guerino, P., Harrison, P. M., & Sabol, W. J. (2011). *Prisoners in 2010* (NCJ 236096). Retrieved from Bureau of Justice Statistics website: http://www.bjs.gov/content/pub/pdf/p10.pdf
9. Glaze, L. E. (2011). *Correctional populations in the United States, 2010* (NCJ 236319). Retrieved from Bureau of Justice Statistics website: http://bjs.ojp.usdoj.gov/content/pub/pdf/cpus10.pdf
10. Fagan, J., & Meares, T. L. (2008). Punishment, deterrence and social control: The paradox of punishment in minority communities. *Ohio State Journal of Criminal Law, 6,* 173–229.
11. Sommers, S. R., & Marotta, S. A. (2014). Racial disparities in legal outcomes on policing, charging decisions, and criminal trial proceedings. *Policy Insights from the Behavioral and Brain Sciences, 1,* 103–111.
12. Mitchell, O. (2005). A meta-analysis of race and sentencing research: Explaining the inconsistencies. *Journal of Quantatative Criminolgy, 21,* 439–466.
13. Fair Sentencing Act of 2010, Pub. L. No. 111-120, 21 U.S.C. § 1789, 124 Stat. 2372 (2010).
14. Tonry, M. (2011). *Punishing race: A continuing American dilemma.* New York, NY: Oxford University Press.
15. Burke, A. S. (2006). Improving prosecutorial decision making: Some lessons of cognitive science. *William & Mary Law Review, 47,* 1587–1633.
16. Smith, A. (2001). Can you be a good person and a good prosecutor? *Georgetown Journal of Legal Ethics, 14,* 355–400.
17. Kutateladze, B., Lynn, V., & Liang, E. (2012). *Do race and ethnicity matter in prosecution? A review of empirical studies.* Retrieved from Vera Institute of Justice website: http://www.vera.org/sites/default/files/resources/downloads/race-and-ethnicity-in-prosecution-first-edition.pdf
18. Johnson, J. L. (2014). *Mass incarceration on trial: A remarkable court decision and the future of prisons in America.* New York, NY: New Press.
19. Henning, K. N. (2013). Criminalizing normal adolescent behavior in communities of color: The role of prosecutors in juvenile justice reform. *Cornell Law Review, 98,* 383–462.

20. Levinson, J. D., & Young, D. (2010). Different shades of bias: Skin tone, implicit racial bias, and judgments of ambiguous evidence. *West Virginia Law Review, 112,* 307–350.

21. Correll, J., Park, B., Judd, C. M., & Wittenbrink, B. (2007). The influence of stereotypes on decisions to shoot. *European Journal of Social Psychology, 37,* 1102–1117.

22. Hartney, C., & Silva, F. (2007). *And justice for some: Differential treatment of youth of color in the justice system.* Retrieved from National Council on Crime and Delinquency website: http://www.nccdglobal.org/sites/default/files/publication_pdf/justice-for-some.pdf

23. Rattan, A., Levine, C. S., Dweck, C. S., Eberhardt, J. L., & Avenanti, A. (2012). Race and the fragility of the legal distinction between juveniles and adults. *PLOS ONE, 7*(5), Article e36680.

24. Goff, P. A., Jackson, M. C., Di Leone, B. A. L., Culotta, C. M., & DiTomasso, N. A. (2014). The essence of innocence: Consequences of dehumanizing Black children. *Journal of Personality and Social Psychology, 106,* 526–545.

25. Sah, S., & Fugh-Berman, A. (2013). Physicians under the influence: Social psychology and industry marketing strategies. *Journal of Law, Medicine and Ethics, 41,* 665–672.

26. Sah, S. (2013). Essays on conflicts of interest in medicine. *Business & Society, 52,* 666–678.

27. Johnson, S. L. (1988). Unconscious racism and the criminal law. *Cornell Law Review, 73,* 1016–1037.

28. Lawrence, C. R. (1987). The id, the ego, and equal protection: Reckoning with unconscious racism. *Stanford Law Review, 38,* 317–388.

29. Babcock, L., & Loewenstein, G. (1997). Explaining bargaining impasse: The role of self-serving biases. *The Journal of Economic Perspectives, 11,* 109–126.

30. Sah, S., & Larrick, R. (2015). *I am immune: A sense of invulnerability predicts increased acceptance of, and influence from, conflicts of interest* (Cornell University Working Papers).

31. Sah, S., & Loewenstein, G. (2010). Effect of reminders of personal sacrifice and suggested rationalizations on residents' self-reported willingness to accept gifts: A randomized trial. *Journal of the American Medical Association, 304,* 1204–1211.

32. Dror, I. E., & Cole, S. A. (2010). The vision in "blind" justice: Expert perception, judgment, and visual cognition in forensic pattern recognition. *Psychonomic Bulletin & Review, 17,* 161–167.

33. Sah, S. (2012). Conflicts of interest and your physician: Psychological processes that cause unexpected changes in behavior. *Journal of Law, Medicine & Ethics, 40,* 482–487.

34. Levinson, J. D. (2007). Forgotten racial equality: Implicit bias, decisionmaking, and misremembering. *Duke Law Journal, 57,* 345–424.

35. Oliver, M. B. (1999). Caucasian viewers' memory of Black and White criminal suspects in the news. *Journal of Communication, 49,* 46–60.

36. Eberhardt, J. L., Davies, P. G., Purdie-Vaughns, V. J., & Johnson, S. L. (2006). Looking deathworthy: Perceived stereotypicality of Black defendants predicts capital-sentencing outcomes. *Psychological Science, 17,* 383–386.

37. Viglione, J., Hannon, L., & DeFina, R. (2011). The impact of light skin on prison time for Black female offenders. *The Social Science Journal, 48,* 250–258.

38. U.S. Department of Justice. (2014). *Guidance for Federal law enforcement agencies regarding the use of race, ethnicity, gender, national origin, religion, sexual orientation, or gender identity.* Retrieved from http://www.justice.gov/sites/default/files/ag/pages/attachments/2014/12/08/use-of-race-policy.pdf

39. Haidt, J. (2001). The emotional dog and its rational tail: A social intuitionist approach to moral judgment. *Psychological Review, 108,* 814–834.

40. Gunia, B. C., Barnes, C. M., & Sah, S. (2014). The morality of larks and owls: Unethical behavior depends on chronotype as well as time of day. *Psychological Science, 25,* 2271–2274.

41. Pronin, E., Lin, D. Y., & Ross, L. (2002). The bias blind spot: Perceptions of bias in self versus others. *Personality and Social Psychology Bulletin, 28,* 369–391.

42. Pronin, E., Gilovich, T., & Ross, L. (2004). Objectivity in the eye of the beholder: Divergent perceptions of bias in self versus others. *Psychological Review, 111,* 781–799.

43. Davis, A. J. (2013). In search of racial justice: The role of the prosecutor. *New York University Journal of Legislation and Public Policy, 16,* 821–851.

44. Sah, S., & Loewenstein, G. (2014). Nothing to declare: Mandatory and voluntary disclosure leads advisors to avoid conflicts of interest. *Psychological Science, 25,* 575–584.

45. Plant, E. A. (2004). Responses to interracial interactions over time. *Personality and Social Psychology Bulletin, 30,* 1458–1471.

46. Rosenthal, R. (1978). How often are our numbers wrong? *American Psychologist, 33,* 1005–1008.

47. Goldin, C., & Rouse, C. (2000). Orchestrating impartiality: The impact of "blind" auditions on female musicians. *The American Economic Review, 90,* 715–741.

48. Schulz, K. F., & Grimes, D. A. (2002). Blinding in randomised trials: Hiding who got what. *The Lancet, 359,* 696–700.

49. Wood, L., Egger, M., Gluud, L. L., Schulz, K. F., Juni, P., Altman, D. G., . . . Sterne, J. A. C. (2008). Empirical evidence of bias in treatment effect estimates in controlled trials with different interventions and outcomes: Meta-epidemiological study. *British Medical Journal, 336,* 601–605.

50. Psaty, B. M., & Prentice, R. L. (2010). Minimizing bias in randomized trials: The importance of blinding. *Journal of the American Medical Association, 304,* 793–794.

51. Snodgrass, R. (2006). Single- versus double-blind reviewing: An analysis of the literature. *ACM SIGMOD Record, 35*(3), 8–21.

52. Carrington, P. D. (1992). One law: The role of legal education in the opening of the legal profession since 1776. *Florida Law Review, 44,* 501–603.

53. Dysart, J. E., Lawson, V. Z., & Rainey, A. (2012). Blind lineup administration as a prophylactic against the postidentification feedback effect. *Law and Human Behavior, 36,* 312–319.

54. Garrett, B. L. (2014). Eyewitness identifications and police practices: A Virginia case study. *Virginia Journal of Criminal Law, 2,* 2013–2026.

55. Wells, G. L. (1988). *Eyewitness identification: A system handbook.* Toronto, Ontario, Canada: Carswell Legal.

56. U.S. Department of Justice, Technical Working Group for Eyewitness Evidence. (1999). *Eyewitness evidence: A guide for law enforcement* (NCJ 178240). Retrieved from https://www.ncjrs.gov/pdffiles1/nij/178240.pdf

57. Famer, J. J. J. (2001, April 18). Attorney general guidelines for preparing and conducting photo and live lineup identification procedures [Letter]. Retrieved from State of New Jersey website: http://www.state.nj.us/lps/dcj/agguide/photoid.pdf

58. National Research Council. (2014). *Identifying the culprit: Assessing eyewitness identification.* Washington, DC: National Academies Press.

59. *Federal Rules of Evidence: Rule 403. Excluding relevant evidence for prejudice, confusion, waste of time, or other reasons.* Retrieved from Legal Information Institute website: https://www.law.cornell.edu/rules/fre/rule_403

60. U.S. Department of Justice. (2001). *The federal death penalty system: Supplementary data, analysis and revised protocol for capital case review.* Retrieved from http://www.justice.gov/archive/dag/pubdoc/deathpenaltystudy.htm

61. Milkman, K. L., Akinola, M., & Chugh, D. (2012). Temporal distance and discrimination: An audit study in academia. *Psychological Science, 23,* 710–717.

62. Sah, S., & Loewenstein, G. (2012). More affected = more neglected: Amplification of bias in advice to the unidentified and many. *Social Psychological and Personality Science, 3,* 365–372.

63. Jensen, R. (2005). *The heart of Whiteness: Confronting race, racism and White privilege.* San Francisco, CA: City Lights Books.

64. Lowery, B. S., Knowles, E. D., & Unzueta, M. M. (2007). Framing inequity safely: Whites' motivated perceptions of racial privilege. *Personality and Social Psychology Bulletin, 33,* 1237–1250.

65. McIntosh, P. (1998). White privilege: Unpacking the invisible knapsack. In P. S. Rothenberg (Ed.), *Race, class, and gender in the United States: An integrated study* (4th ed., pp. 165–169). New York, NY: Worth.

66. United States Department of Justice, Civil Rights Division. (2015). *Investigation of the Ferguson Police Department.* Retrieved from http://www.justice.gov/sites/default/files/opa/press-releases/attachments/2015/03/04/ferguson_police_department_report.pdf

67. Loewenstein, G., Sah, S., & Cain, D. M. (2012). The unintended consequences of conflict of interest disclosure. *Journal of the American Medical Association, 307,* 669–670. doi:10.1001/jama.2012.154

68. Sah, S., & Loewenstein, G. (2015). Conflicted advice and second opinions: Benefits, but unintended consequences. *Organizational Behavior and Human Decision Processes, 130,* 89–107.

69. Sah, S., Loewenstein, G., & Cain, D. M. (2013). The burden of disclosure: Increased compliance with distrusted advice. *Journal of Personality and Social Psychology, 104,* 289–304.

70. Bertrand, M., & Mullainathan, S. (2004). Are Emily and Greg more employable than Lakisha and Jamal? A field experiment on labor market discrimination. *The American Economic Review, 94,* 991–1013.

71. Kutateladze, B. L., & Andiloro, N. R. (2014). *Prosecution and racial justice in New York County—Technical report* (Technical Report 247227). Retrieved from National Criminal Justice Reference Service website: https://www.ncjrs.gov/pdffiles1/nij/grants/247227.pdf

72. Gershowitz, A. M., & Killinger, L. (2011). The state (never) rests: How excessive prosecutor caseloads harm criminal defendants. *Northwestern University Law Review, 105,* 262–301.

73. Perry, S., & Banks, D. (2011). *Prosecutors in state courts—2007 statistical tables* (NCJ 234211). Retrieved from Bureau of Justice Statistics website: http://www.bjs.gov/content/pub/pdf/psc07st.pdf

74. U.S. Department of Justice. (2011). *United States attorneys' annual statistical report: Fiscal year 2010.* Retrieved from http://www.justice.gov/sites/default/files/usao/legacy/2011/09/01/10statrpt.pdf

75. Rosenmerkel, S., Durose, M., & Farole, D., Jr. (2009). *Felony sentences in state courts, 2006—Statistical tables* (NCJ 226846). Retrieved from Bureau of Justice Statistics website: http://www.bjs.gov/content/pub/pdf/fssc06st.pdf

76. Schmitt, J., Warner, K., & Gupta, S. (2010). *The high budgetary cost of incarceration.* Retrieved from Center for Economic and Policy Research website: http://www.cepr.net/publications/reports/the-high-budgetary-cost-of-incarceration

77. Western, B., & Pettit, B. (2010). *Collateral costs: Incarceration's effect on economic mobility.* Retrieved from Pew Charitable Trusts website: http://www.pewtrusts.org/~/media/legacy/uploadedfiles/pcs_assets/2010/collateralcosts1pdf.pdf

78. Tyler, T. R. (1990). *Why people obey the law: Procedural justice, legitimacy, and compliance.* New Haven, CT: Yale University Press.

The White House Social & Behavioral Sciences Team: Lessons learned from year one

William J. Congdon and Maya Shankar

Summary. On September 15, 2015, President Obama signed Executive Order 13707 titled "Using Behavioral Science Insights to Better Serve the American People." The order directs federal agencies to integrate behavioral insights into their policies and programs and formally establishes the Social and Behavioral Sciences Team (SBST). Originally launched in 2014, SBST translates insights from behavioral science research into improvements in federal policies and programs. In its first annual report, SBST detailed results from projects that drew on behavioral insights to promote retirement security, expand college access and affordability, connect workers and small businesses with economic opportunities, improve health outcomes, and increase program integrity and government efficiency. The results of SBST projects offer important lessons for bringing a behavioral perspective to federal policy. The executive order provides a framework for future policy applications.

In 2014, the White House Office of Science and Technology Policy created the Social and Behavioral Sciences Team (SBST) to translate research findings and methods from the social and behavioral sciences into improvements in federal policies and programs for the benefit of the American people. Building on SBST's first year of work, President Obama signed Executive Order 13707, "Using Behavioral Science Insights to Better Serve the American People," on September 15, 2015.[1] The order directs federal agencies to integrate behavioral insights into their policies and programs and formally establishes SBST.

The third paragraph of Executive Order 13707 perhaps best articulates SBST's goals:

> To more fully realize the benefits of behavioral insights and deliver better results at a lower cost for the American people, the Federal Government should design its policies and programs to reflect our best understanding of how people engage with, participate in, use, and respond to those policies and programs. By improving the effectiveness and efficiency of Government,

Congdon, W. J., & Shankar, M. (2015). The White House Social & Behavioral Sciences Team: Lessons learned from year one. *Behavioral Science & Policy, 1*(2).

behavioral science insights can support a range of national priorities, including helping workers to find better jobs; enabling Americans to lead longer, healthier lives; improving access to educational opportunities and support for success in school; and accelerating the transition to a low-carbon economy.

SBST strives to achieve these goals by identifying federal policy and program objectives that depend on the decisions or actions of individuals. It then leverages insights from behavioral science research to redesign those policies and programs accordingly. Successful SBST projects to date demonstrate that behavioral science research can help government programs better serve Americans.

SBST projects have implications for policymakers throughout government, as well as for behavioral science researchers in academia and elsewhere. By virtue of its wide array of programs and the scale at which those programs operate, the U.S. federal government is in a unique position to realize the potential social payoffs from behaviorally informed policymaking. Policymakers, program administrators, and behavioral science researchers all share a stake in the success of this initiative.

Results from SBST's initial projects offer some early lessons for developing behavioral applications to federal policy. Below, we explore a few of those lessons. We also expand upon the framework of Executive Order 13707, which builds on some of the early work and provides direction for future policy applications of behavioral science research.

Lessons from SBST's First Year of Work

SBST's first year was a demonstration of proof of concept. The goal was to show that the federal government could launch a coordinated effort that effectively applied behavioral science insights to a range of federal government programs. In September 2015, SBST released its first annual report, which detailed the results of a set of initial projects that drew on behavioral insights. These projects helped promote retirement security, expand college access and affordability, connect workers and small businesses with economic opportunities, improve health outcomes, and increase program integrity and government efficiency.[2] (See

Table 1 at the end of this article for brief descriptions of the projects.) Several important lessons emerged from this initial portfolio of collaborations, including those illustrated by the four case studies described below.

The Case for Change Is Cumulative

In its first year, SBST focused on executing projects in which behavioral insights could be embedded directly into programs at a low cost and potentially generate immediate, quantifiable improvements in program outcomes. Given the short time frame, most large policy design features, such as default settings of policy choices, were taken as fixed. That said, these quick, small-scale projects set the stage for larger projects and collaborations down the line.

A sequence of collaborations with the Department of Defense (DOD) promoting retirement security illustrates this point. In 2014, only 42% of active duty service members—compared with 87% of civilian federal employees—were enrolled in the Thrift Savings Plan (TSP), the federal government's workplace savings program. One likely cause for this difference is that the federal government automatically enrolls civilian employees in TSP, but has not done so with service members (a practice due to change in 2018).

Given the extensive body of behavioral science research that addresses retirement savings, SBST identified this policy area as a ripe opportunity to apply behavioral insights.[3,4] To quickly demonstrate the impact of behavioral insights on DOD programs and to gain momentum in support of future large-scale efforts, SBST and DOD looked first for a chance to rapidly implement a low-cost, quantifiable behavioral intervention.

SBST identified one such opportunity in December 2014, when DOD indicated that it planned to send out an e-mail notice to approximately 140,000 service members enrolled in a Roth TSP, a type of TSP plan. The notice alerted service members of a change in the online military pay system that would require them to reenroll in their Roth TSP in January 2015 to avoid having their contributions suspended indefinitely. SBST worked with DOD to leverage behavioral insights to redesign the notice and to embed a low-cost, randomized evaluation into a broader outreach campaign. The redesigned version of the e-mail emphasized the New Year as a chance for service members to make a fresh start with their finances, clarified the steps needed to complete the reenrollment process, and encouraged action to avoid losing the chance to contribute savings.[5]

Within one week of the e-mails being sent, the redesigned e-mail using behavioral insights led to a 5.2-percentage-point increase (from 23.5% to 28.7%) in reenrollments in the Roth TSP relative to the original notice. On the basis of this result, DOD scaled up the effective behavioral messaging in follow-up email messages to all service members that encouraged them to act before the reenrollment deadline.

More important, on the basis of this initial pilot study and its demonstration that behavioral insights were a low-cost, effective tool for supporting DOD's goal of service member financial security, DOD entered into a larger-scale, multiyear collaboration with SBST. Over the course of 2015, DOD and SBST collaborated on two additional projects. The first was a pilot study that prompted service members not enrolled in TSP to make a yes or no choice about whether to sign up for TSP during an orientation briefing upon their arrival at a new military base. This pilot study led to a significant boost in TSP enrollments.[4] The second was an e-mail campaign that sent approximately 720,000 nonenrolled service members messages about TSP that were designed using behavioral insights: these insights included framing the decision to enroll as a choice between two options ("Yes, I want to enroll" or "No, I do not want to enroll") and charting out clear action steps for enrolling.[6] In this campaign, messages informed by behavioral insights led to roughly 4,930 new enrollments and $1.3 million in savings in just the first month after the messages were sent.

On the basis of the success of these efforts, SBST and DOD continue to expand the scope of this work. DOD has committed to applying insights from the military base pilot study to bases and installations across the country with higher troop concentrations. Moreover, DOD now sends service members periodic e-mails informed by behavioral insights about the benefits of TSP. (In an action independent of the efforts described above, Congress in 2015 passed legislation that will require that new service members be automatically enrolled in TSP beginning in 2018.)

Pilot Studies Are Only Starting Points

Although SBST conducts much of its work as empirical projects, research is not its end goal. Demonstration projects and evaluations are merely ways to identify whether an intervention has an effect and to develop evidence for how to better design programs and policies. Ensuring that policies and programs incorporate the lessons of those empirical projects requires independent attention and effort.

A project with the General Services Administration (GSA) demonstrates this point. When the government purchases goods and services from vendors under certain contracts, those vendors are required to do two things: first, report those sales to the government and, second, pay a small fraction of their reported sales to the federal government as an administrative fee known as the Industrial Funding Fee (IFF).

To promote more accurate self-reporting of the sales and, consequently, more accurate payments of the IFF, SBST and GSA introduced a required signature box at the top of an online payment form for a random sample of roughly 18,000 contractors. The signature box asked contractors to confirm the truth and accuracy of the information they were about to report. This intervention is based on research showing that requiring people to sign their names to confirm the accuracy of self-reported statements at the top of a form can reduce self-reporting errors.[7]

Results demonstrated that the signature box at the top of the form was effective. The median self-reported sales amount was $445 higher for vendors signing at the top of the form compared with those vendors who were not required to make this confirmation. The combined amounts collected totaled $28.6 million from those for whom the confirmation was required, compared with $27.0 million from those for whom it was not. In other words, by introducing the signature box, the federal government collected an additional $1.59 million in fees in a single quarter.

Although this was an exciting result, crucially, the work of SBST did not end there. SBST continued its collaboration with GSA to help bring this pilot study's result to scale. GSA is now making permanent changes to the online form to incorporate a signature box so that it can achieve improved IFF program integrity on an ongoing basis.

Testing Is Feasible, Effective, and Informative

At its core, SBST's mandate is one of translation: using promising research findings to create pragmatic program solutions. But designing optimal ways to communicate with the public, to structure choices and incentives, and to help qualifying individuals access public programs is not as simple as reviewing the scientific literature and implementing its findings. Decades of behavioral research has shown that the ways in which individuals respond to program details, such as the presentation of information or the structure of choices, is highly context specific.

As a result, any effort to translate behavioral research to policy will benefit from frequent evaluation and feedback. Whenever possible, SBST works with agencies to rigorously test the impact of behavioral insights on program outcomes before implementing them widely. In this way, SBST can learn about what works, what works best, and what does not work. Moreover, because agencies can often embed these tests directly into their programs and evaluate impacts using existing administrative data, the tests can be relatively quick and inexpensive.[8,9] Two null results from projects in SBST's first year illustrate the importance of this approach. In both cases, SBST and agency collaborators leveraged research showing that highlighting the contrast between the actions of an individual and the social norm (how most people act) can successfully prompt action.[10,11]

In one project, SBST worked with the Department of the Treasury's Debt Management Service (DMS) to increase collections from individuals with outstanding nontax debt. Individuals might incur this type of debt by, for example, failing to repay Medicare for an overpayment they received. SBST and DMS redesigned DMS's standard collection letter to include simplified language, a shortened web address for making online payments, a personalized salutation, and a prominent reference to the total amount owed in the letter's opening line. It also included an accurate statement that 91% of Americans pay their debts on time (appealing to a social norm of timely payments).[12]

DMS sent approximately 21,000 letters to debtors. There was no observed difference in payment rates between those who were sent the redesigned collection letter and those who were sent the standard collection letter. The age and status of this debt may have been contributing factors. Recipients of these letters were already 180 days or more behind in their payments.

The second project involved the Centers for Medicare and Medicaid Services' (CMS's) efforts to combat inappropriate drug prescribing. Drawing again on social norms, SBST and CMS produced a letter sent to a subset of providers with unusually high billing patterns for Schedule II prescriptions such as opioids. Each letter compared the recipient's prescribing rates with those of his or her peers and provided educational information about proper prescribing practices. No measurable impact on prescription rates was seen over the 90 days after the letter was mailed.[13] On the basis of this finding, CMS and SBST are implementing additional approaches to reducing overprescribing that will alter the design, timing, and frequency of the government's letters.

Results Build Evidence for Broader Changes

To serve its mission, SBST ensures its projects always include the goal of supporting broader conclusions about ways to improve the operations of government, the administration of federal programs, or the design of federal policies. This goes beyond simply applying the direct results of a test to a program or adopting interventions that work and abandoning those that do not. In many cases, the success or failure of a particular intervention can inform decisions about broader policy changes.

One example comes from a project with the Department of Veterans Affairs (VA). The goal was to expand veterans' access to benefits designed to help service members successfully reintegrate into civilian society. Through its Chapter 36 benefits program, the VA offers a variety of education, training, and job placement services.

SBST worked with the VA to increase awareness and participation in this benefits program with low-cost informational e-mails. The VA sent veterans either one of two e-mails or no e-mail (the business-as-usual practice).[14,15] One e-mail highlighted veterans' eligibility for the benefit; the other e-mail highlighted that veterans had *earned* the benefit through their years of service. The e-mail emphasizing that the benefit was earned led to more action; nearly 9% more veterans who received it clicked through to the benefit application than did those who received the e-mail that simply emphasized that they were eligible.

Still, the number of benefit applications that veterans filled out remained quite low. Between November 2014 (when the e-mails were sent) and March 2015, only 146 veterans (0.3% of the people who received e-mails) applied for Chapter 36 benefits. The results suggest that barriers to enrollment in the Chapter 36 benefit program lie elsewhere and that more extensive changes may be necessary to promote access to these benefits. Results such as these can compel deeper analysis into the true barriers that may limit access to or effective engagement with government programs.

Even in instances where a light-touch intervention is effective, SBST results can suggest potentially more ambitious changes to program and policy designs. For example, if prompting service member enrollment in a retirement savings plan at key points during service member careers can significantly boost participation, what might that mean for how access to that plan should be designed in the first place? If a single informational e-mail can help individuals choose a student loan repayment program, what might this suggest about how best to structure that choice set? Through small changes to program administration, the impacts of SBST projects point to broader opportunities for policymakers to use behavioral insights to achieve policy goals across the federal government.

Future Directions under the Executive Order

In addition to the directives described above, Executive Order 13707 provides a high-level framework for identifying elements of policies, programs, and operations where behavioral insights might strongly contribute to desired policy outcomes.[16-20] This framework provides a point of departure for policymakers who seek to apply research insights from behavioral science to current policy challenges. In doing so, it also provides a potentially instructive point of reference to behavioral science researchers outside of government regarding avenues of investigation or research questions that are most directly and immediately policy relevant. Below we elaborate on how SBST interprets this framework.

Rules and Procedures Governing Access to Programs

The order encourages agencies to "identify opportunities to help qualifying individuals, families, communities, and businesses access programs and benefits" (see reference 1, section 1[b][i]). Behavioral science research demonstrates that seemingly small barriers to program access—such as lengthy or complex applications—can limit participation in programs by eligible individuals.[21]

Further, a behavioral perspective suggests that complex eligibility criteria may in some instances impose costs to program access that outweigh the benefits of improved targeting efficiency. For example, research indicates not only that the complexity of the application for federal student aid deters some students from enrolling in college.[22] It also provides evidence that basing aid determinations on less information about financial aid applicants would have modest effect on the program's goal of providing aid to people who need it most.[23] Together these results provide important evidence regarding the optimal design not just of the application process, but also of the underlying eligibility criteria that determine student aid amounts.

The order's emphasis on access also highlights the value of research examining behavioral determinants of participation in federal programs. The success and impact of the policy applications of research on financial aid applications and retirement plan participation follow, in part, from the direct policy relevance of that research.[22,3]

Provision of Information

Agencies are encouraged to "improve how information is presented to consumers, borrowers, program beneficiaries, and other individuals" (see reference 1, section 1[b][ii]). Many federal policies provide, require, or set standards for the provision of information to the public to help inform individual decisions. A behavioral perspective emphasizes the importance of presenting information in ways that are meaningful to individuals and allow for the effective use of that information.

For this reason, research into how behavioral factors interact with the content and presentation of information provided or regulated by federal agencies is valuable for policy. To take one example, research shows that individuals are better able to form accurate judgments about automotive fuel efficiency when information is presented as gallons per mile rather than miles per gallon. This research has directly informed the design of the sticker required by the Environmental Protection Agency on new cars.[24,25]

Presentation and Structure of Choices Offered by Programs and Policies

The order encourages agencies to "identify programs that offer choices and carefully consider how the presentation and structure of those choices . . . can most effectively promote public welfare" (see reference

1, section 1[b][iii]). In situations where federal programs offer individuals choices, a behavioral perspective emphasizes how contextual factors, such as the complexity of choices or the number of options, are likely to influence decisions.[26]

Behavioral insights can address important issues related to program choice not just by simplifying the presentation of or assisting with those choices, but also by streamlining the number of options or the dimensionality of choice attributes. Behavioral insights can also help in situations where individuals are not presented with explicit menus of program choices but still have options in how they use programs—for example, the choice of when to claim a benefit.

The order's emphasis on choice also highlights the value of continued behavioral science research on the construction of choice sets and the presentation of choices in federal programs. Examples include research on choices among health insurance plans offered by programs such as Medicare[27,28] or research exploring how people choose when to claim retirement benefits in Social Security.[29]

Use of Incentives to Achieve Policy Objectives

Finally, agencies are urged to "review elements of their policies and programs that are designed to encourage . . . specific actions, such as saving for retirement or completing education programs" (see reference 1, section 1[b][iv]). A central insight from behavioral science is that individuals do not respond to financial incentives as neatly as predicted by, for example, standard economic theory.[30,31] In addition, individuals respond, sometimes strongly, to nonprice or nonfinancial incentives.[17,32]

Behavioral insights point to how the salience, structure, and timing of financial incentives can mediate their effectiveness.[33] In addition, research from behavioral science reveals instances when nonfinancial incentives may be more effective or efficient than financial incentives. For example, research has shown that automatic enrollment is, in some contexts, more effective at encouraging savings in retirement savings plans than tax incentives are.[34]

The order's emphasis on incentives also highlights the value of research aimed at understanding behavioral responses to the incentives created by federal policies.

One example is research demonstrating that some individuals may be more responsive to tax incentives to save for retirement if the benefit is structured as a match to savings rather than as a tax credit.[35,36]

Next Steps for Program Officials, Researchers, and Policymakers

SBST's work to date has produced improvements in outcomes across a range of federal policy areas. But in many ways, it illustrates just how much more work there is to be done, by researchers and policymakers alike, before the sustained translation of behavioral science insights into federal policy reaches its full potential. Identifying and realizing these broader applications will be ongoing work and involve the continued and collaborative engagement of program officials, policymakers, and researchers.

For program officials who are working to apply behavioral insights at various levels of government, the lessons of SBST's first year are possibly instructive: Quick proof-of-concept work can build momentum for larger efforts, but lasting program and policy changes remain the end goal for this initiative. Agency officials may find it especially productive to look for opportunities to apply behavioral science insights to improve outcomes when they are administering or implementing rules that govern program access, offer choices, present information, or provide incentives.

For researchers, the framework laid out by the executive order provides a view into the elements of federal policies and programs where behavioral science research is likely to be most immediately and directly relevant. In this context, the order suggests questions for future research. For example, what can behavioral science teach policymakers about how to ensure that income-support programs reach their intended beneficiaries efficiently? How should policymakers provide consumers with information that help them make energy-saving choices among appliances, automobiles, or homes? How can we most effectively structure choices for borrowers among student loan repayment plans? The list of open questions remains long.

Researchers should also continue to seek opportunities to work with the federal government directly on applications of their research to policy. The order calls on agencies to both "recruit behavioral science

Table 1. Results from the Social and Behavioral Sciences Team 2015 Annual Report

Project	Description	Result
Service member Thrift Savings Plan (TSP) enrollment campaign	To promote participation in TSP, a workplace savings plan, SBST and the Department of Defense (DOD) launched an e-mail campaign. The DOD sent approximately 720,000 not-enrolled service members one of nine e-mails, with messages that applied various behavioral insights such as framing the decision to enroll as a choice between two options ("Yes, I want to enroll" or "No, I do not want to enroll").[6]	Compared with no message, the most effective message nearly doubled the rate at which service members signed up for TSP. E-mails informed by behavioral insights led to roughly 4,930 new enrollments and $1.3 million in savings in just one month. DOD is scaling up this intervention by sending periodic e-mails informed by behavioral insights to service members about the benefits of TSP.
TSP enrollment on base	To further promote saving, SBST and DOD prompted service members to make a yes or no choice about whether to contribute to TSP during an orientation briefing upon their arrival at a new military base. This intervention drew on research finding that asking employees to actively choose whether to participate in workplace savings plans can increase enrollment.[4]	The number of service members enrolling in TSP increased during the prompted-choice pilot study: 8.7% of nonenrolled service members enrolled, compared with 2.9% on average at three comparison bases and 4.3% during comparison periods at the pilot study's base. On the basis of that success, DOD intends to apply insights from this pilot study across bases and installations with higher troop concentrations.
Roth TSP reenrollment	To assist nearly 140,000 service members who were required to reenroll in their Roth TSP to continue making contributions, SBST and DOD redesigned an e-mail that alerted service members to the requirement to reenroll, incorporating behavioral insights such as emphasizing the new year as a chance for service members to make a fresh start.[5]	The redesigned e-mail led 22% more service members to reenroll in TSP within a week—3,770 more reenrollments than among those sent a standard message. On the basis of this result, DOD immediately scaled up the successful messaging in subsequent outreach efforts to remind service members to reenroll in TSP.
Curbing college enrollment summer melt	To help students enroll in college, SBST and the Department of Education's office of Federal Student Aid (FSA) provided technical expertise to researchers and the nonprofit uAspire on the crafting of messages notifying high school graduates accepted to college of tasks required for matriculation. This trial built on prior work showing that sending students low-cost text message reminders to complete such tasks can curb summer melt.[37]	A series of eight personalized text messages to low-income students reminding them to complete the required tasks led to a 5.7-percentage-point increase in college enrollment, from 66.4% to 72.1%.
Student loan payment reminders	To help federal student loan borrowers repay those loans, SBST and FSA sent a reminder e-mail to over 100,000 borrowers who had missed their first payments. Research from other contexts suggests that low-cost reminders of this nature can help individuals make payments.[38-40]	In the first week after it was sent, the reminder e-mail led to a 29.6% increase in the fraction of borrowers making a payment, moving the total from 2.7% to 3.5%.
Income-driven student loan repayment	To increase awareness of income-driven repayment (IDR) plans among student loan borrowers, SBST and FSA sent an informational e-mail about IDR plans to more than 800,000 borrowers who had fallen behind on payments. This project built on research finding that timely notices increase the use of benefits such as tax credits.[41]	The low-cost, timely message led to a fourfold increase in applications for IDR plans, with 4,327 applications for IDR plans made within 20 days of the e-mail being sent.
Education and career counseling veterans benefits	To increase veterans' use of education and career counseling benefits, SBST and the Department of Veterans Affairs sent notices informing veterans of their benefits and the steps needed to apply.	Highlighting that the veterans had earned the benefits led nearly 9% more veterans within the sample to access the application for the benefits.[14,15]
Microloans for farmers	To improve economic outcomes for small-scale and specialized farmers, SBST and the United States Department of Agriculture (USDA) collaborated on a campaign to increase knowledge and use of loan options.	Farms that were sent a personalized letter with a customized set of action steps for applying for a microloan were 22% more likely to obtain a loan, increasing from 0.09 to 0.11%.

(continued

Project	Description	Result
Federal health insurance marketplace enrollment	To assist individuals and families with obtaining health insurance, SBST and the Department of Health and Human Services (HHS) sent one of eight behaviorally designed letter variants to each of more than 700,000 individuals who had already begun but not completed the enrollment process. The letters varied behavioral dynamics, including action language, an implementation intention prompt, a picture, social norm messaging, a pledge, and loss aversion.[10,42–44]	Those sent the most effective version of the letter were 13.2% more likely to enroll in health insurance than were those not sent a letter, with enrollment rates of 4.56% and 4.03%, respectively.
Industrial funding fee reports	To improve the accuracy of sales figures self-reported by vendors selling goods and services to the government, SBST and the General Services Administration (GSA) redesigned an online data-entry form to include a signature box at the top of the page where a user had to confirm the accuracy of self-reported sales. This intervention was based on research finding that a confirmation entered at the beginning of a form reduces self-reporting errors.[7]	Because vendors pay the federal government a small fee based on those sales reports, introducing this box led to an additional $1.59 million in fees collected within a single quarter. On the basis of this result, GSA is making permanent changes to the form to incorporate a signature box.
Delinquent debt repayment	To increase debt recovery from individuals with outstanding nontax debt, SBST worked with the Department of the Treasury's Debt Management Service (DMS) to redesign a collection letter. On the basis of recent research from the United Kingdom showing that social comparisons can increase tax collection revenues, the new letter highlighted the fact that 91% of Americans pay their debts on time.[11,12]	No difference in payment rates was observed, but changes such as shortening the web address for making an online payment led 45% more individuals to pay online, representing an increase from 1.5% to 2.2%. DMS has permanently shortened the web link in the collection letter.
Letters to controlled-substance prescribers	To reduce inappropriate prescribing of controlled substances, SBST and HHS's Centers for Medicare and Medicaid Services (CMS) sent providers with unusually high billing patterns a letter comparing their prescribing rates with prescribing rates of their peers. Educational information about proper prescribing practices was included. This intervention was based on research showing that physicians respond to normative messages, for example, receiving feedback on their vaccination rates relative to those of their peers.[45]	No measurable impact was seen on prescription rates.[13]
Moving Treasury accounts online	To determine if letters could encourage security holders to transfer accounts to an online platform, SBST collaborated with the Department of the Treasury's Bureau of the Fiscal Service to design outreach to account holders.	Letters that included a personal appointment made with a call center led to 23% higher call-in rates than standard letters did, representing an increase from 10.6% to 13.0%. The default appointment intervention builds on behavioral science research finding that individuals are more likely to follow through on plans that identify specific moments of action.[46] Account conversion rates remained low for both groups, however.
Tenant satisfaction survey	To increase response rates to a workplace survey that is used to determine federal office space management strategies, SBST and the GSA incorporated behavioral insights into the timing and messaging of e-mails announcing the survey.	Among other findings, e-mail click rates were highest at lunchtime, with 15.3% of e-mails sent at 11:55 a.m. resulting in recipients clicking through to the survey, compared with 13.3% click-through from the 8:55 a.m. letters.
Double-sided printing	To encourage double-sided printing, SBST and the USDA's Economic Research Service (ERS) created a dialog box that asked employees to change their default printer setting to double-sided after employees had initiated a single-sided print job.	This prompt increased the likelihood of double-sided printing by 5.8 percentage points, from a baseline of 46%. On the basis of this finding, ERS plans to change the default setting of all printers to double-sided.

The SBST 2015 report is available at https://sbst.gov/assets/files/2015-annual-report.pdf

experts" and to "strengthen agency relationships with the research community" (see reference 1, section 1[a] [iii–iv]). SBST is eager to foster relationships and collaborations between agencies and the behavioral science research community. Direct engagement with agencies and programs is often the best way for researchers to understand the details of programs and identify feasible behavioral recommendations.

For policymakers, the work of SBST and the executive order point to the potential for still broader social impact. Policy applications of behavioral insights to date, as illustrated by the examples above, have been primarily retrospective. They involve reviewing existing programs through a behavioral science lens and updating programs and policies to reflect recent advances from the field. Going forward, this work should be done on a more prospective basis: Behavioral science findings and methods should be incorporated into policy design as policies are being developed so that they reflect those insights from the start. In other words, much work remains to be done.

author affiliation

Congdon and Shankar, Social and Behavioral Sciences Team. Corresponding author's e-mail address: sbst@gsa.gov

author note

This paper draws heavily on the 2015 Social and Behavioral Sciences Team Annual Report, and the findings reported here reflect the work of the entire Social and Behavioral Sciences Team, as well as agency and program officials across the federal government who collaborated on this work. Any errors or oversights in this paper are, of course, the responsibility of the authors alone.

References

1. Exec. Order No. 13707, 3 C.F.R. 56365–56367 (2015). Retrieved from http://www.gpo.gov/fdsys/pkg/FR-2015-09-18/pdf/2015-23630.pdf
2. Social and Behavioral Sciences Team. (2015). *Annual report*. Retrieved from https://sbst.gov/assets/files/2015-annual-report.pdf
3. Madrian, B. C., & Shea, D. F. (2001). The power of suggestion: Inertia in 401(k) participation and savings behavior. *Quarterly Journal of Economics, 116,* 1149–1187.
4. Carroll, G. D., Choi, J. J., Laibson, D., Madrian, B. C., & Metrick, A. (2009). Optimal defaults and active decisions. *Quarterly Journal of Economics, 124,* 1639–1674.
5. Dai, H., Milkman, K. L., & Riis, J. (2014). The fresh start effect: Temporal landmarks motivate aspirational behavior. *Management Science, 60,* 2563–2582.
6. Putnam-Farr, E., & Riis, J. (2015). *"Yes, I want to enroll": Yes/no response formats increase response rates in marketing communications* (University of Pennsylvania working paper).
7. Shu, L. L., Mazar, N., Gino, F., Ariely, D., & Bazerman, M. H. (2012). Signing at the beginning makes ethics salient and decreases dishonest self-reports in comparison to signing at the end. *Proceedings of the National Academy of Sciences, USA, 109,* 15197–15200.
8. Cody, S., Perez-Johnson, I., & Joyce, K. (2015). Administrative experiments: Unlocking what works better and what works for whom. *American Journal of Evaluation.* Advance online publication. doi:10.1177/1098214015600784
9. Simon, H. A., & Divine, W. R. (1941). Controlling human factors in an administrative experiment. *Public Administration Review, 1,* 485–492.
10. Allcott, H. (2011). Social norms and energy conservation. *Journal of Public Economics, 95,* 1082–1095.
11. Hallsworth, M., List, J. A., Metcalfe, R. D., & Vlaev, I. (2014). *The behavioralist as tax collector: Using natural field experiments to enhance tax compliance* (NBER Working Paper 20007). Retrieved from National Bureau of Economic Research website: http://www.nber.org/papers/w20007
12. "91 percent of Americans..." calculated based on data available at: newyorkfed.org/householdcredit/2013-Q1/data/xls/HHD_C_Report_2013Q1.xlsx
13. Sacarny, A., Yokum, D., Finkelstein, A., & Agrawal, S. (Forthcoming). Reducing inappropriate prescribing of controlled substances in Medicare Part D: Evidence from a randomized intervention. *Health Affairs.*
14. Kahneman, D., Knetsch, J. L., & Thaler, R. H. (1990). Experimental tests of the endowment effect and the Coase theorem. *Journal of Political Economy, 98,* 1325–1348.
15. Hossain, T., & List, J. A. (2012). The behavioralist visits the factory: Increasing productivity using simple framing manipulations. *Management Science, 58,* 2151–2167.
16. Chetty, R. (2015). Behavioral economics and public policy: A pragmatic perspective. *American Economic Review, 105,* 1–33.
17. Madrian, B. C. (2014). Applying insights from behavioral economics to policy design. *Annual Review of Economics, 6,* 663–688.
18. Shafir, E. (Ed.). (2012). *The behavioral foundations of public policy.* Princeton, NJ: Princeton University Press.
19. Congdon, W. J., Kling, J. R., & Mullainathan, S. (2011). *Policy and choice: Public finance through the lens of behavioral economics.* Washington, DC: Brookings Institution Press.
20. Bhargava, S., & Loewenstein, G. (2015). Behavioral Economics and Public Policy 102: Beyond nudging. *American Economic Review, 105,* 396–401.
21. Bertrand, M., Mullainathan, S., & Shafir, E. (2006). Behavioral economics and marketing in aid of decision making among the poor. *Journal of Public Policy & Marketing, 25,* 8–23.
22. Bettinger, E. P., Long, B. T., Oreopoulos, P, & Sanbonmatsu, L. (2012). The role of application assistance and information in college decisions: Results from the H&R Block Fafsa experiment. *Quarterly Journal of Economics, 127,* 1205–1242.
23. Dynarski, S. M., & Scott-Clayton, J. E. (2007). *College grants on a postcard: A proposal for simple and predictable federal student aid* (Hamilton Project Discussion Paper 2007-01). Washington, DC: Brookings Institution.
24. Larrick, R. P., & Soll, J. B. (2008, June 20). The MPG illusion. *Science, 320,* 1593–1594.

25. Sunstein, C. R. (2013). *Simpler: The future of government.* New York, NY: Simon & Schuster.

26. Johnson, E. J., Shu, S. B., Dellaert, B. G. C., Fox, C., Goldstein, D. G., Häubl, G., . . . Weber, E. U. (2012). Beyond nudges: Tools of a choice architecture. *Marketing Letters, 23,* 487–504.

27. Kling, J. R., Mullainathan, S., Shafir, E., Vermeulen, L. C., & Wrobel, M. V. (2012). Comparison friction: Experimental evidence from Medicare drug plans. *The Quarterly Journal of Economics, 127,* 199–235.

28. Ubel, P. A., Comerford, D. A., & Johnson, E. (2015). Healthcare. gov 3.0—Behavioral economics and insurance exchanges. *New England Journal of Medicine, 372,* 695–698.

29. Liebman, J. B., & Luttmer, E. F. P. (2015). Would people behave differently if they better understood Social Security? Evidence from a field experiment. *American Economic Journal: Economic Policy, 7,* 275–299.

30. Gneezy, U., Meier, S., & Rey-Biel, P. (2011, Fall). When and why incentives (don't) work to modify behavior. *Journal of Economic Perspectives, 25*(4), 191–210.

31. Kamenica, E. (2012). Behavioral economics and psychology of incentives. *Annual Review of Economics, 4,* 427–452.

32. Thaler, R. H., & Sunstein, C. R. (2008). *Nudge: Improving decisions about health, wealth, and happiness.* New Haven, CT: Yale University Press.

33. Chetty, R., Looney, A., & Kroft, K. (2009). Salience and taxation: Theory and evidence. *American Economic Review,* 99, 1145–77.

34. Chetty, R., Friedman, J. N., Leth-Petersen, S., Nielsen, T. H., & Olsen, T. (2014). Active vs. passive decisions and crowd-out in retirement savings accounts: Evidence from Denmark. *Quarterly Journal of Economics, 129,* 1141–1219.

35. Duflo, E., Gale, W., Liebman, J., Orszag, P., & Saez, E. (2006). Saving incentives for low- and middle-income families: Evidence from a field experiment with H&R Block. *Quarterly Journal of Economics, 121,* 1311–1346.

36. Saez, E. (2009). Details matter: The impact of presentation and information on the take-up of financial incentives for retirement saving. *American Economic Journal: Economic Policy, 1,* 204–228.

37. Castleman, B. J., & Page, L. C. (2015). Summer nudging: Can personalized text messages and peer mentor outreach increase college going among low-income high school graduates? *Journal of Economic Behavior & Organization, 115,* 144–160.

38. Karlan, D., McConnell, M., Mullainathan, S., & Zinman, J. (2016). Getting to the top of mind: How reminders increase saving. *Management Science.* January. doi:10.1287/mnsc.2015.2296

39. Cadena, X., & Schoar, A. (2011). *Remembering to pay? Reminders vs. financial incentives for loan payments* (NBER Working Paper 17020). Available from National Bureau of Economic Research website: http://www.nber.org/papers/w17020

40. Baird, P., Reardon, L., Cullinan, D., McDermott, D., & Landers, P. (2015). *Reminders to pay: Using behavioral economics to increase child support payments* (OPRE Report 2015-20). Washington, DC: Office of Planning, Research and Evaluation, Administration for Children and Families, U.S. Department of Health and Human Services.

41. Bhargava, S., & Manoli, D. (2015). Psychological frictions and the incomplete take-up of social benefits: Evidence from an IRS field experiment. *American Economic Review, 105,* 3489–3529.

42. Milkman, K. L., Beshears, J., Choi, J. J., Laibson, D., & Madrian, B. C. (2011). Using implementation intentions prompts to enhance influenza vaccination rates. *Proceedings of the National Academy of Sciences, USA, 108,* 10415–10420.

43. Bertrand, M., Mullainathan, S., Shafir, E., & Zinman, J. (2010). What's advertising content worth? Evidence from a consumer credit marketing field experiment. *Quarterly Journal of Economics, 125,* 263–306.

44. Kahneman, D., & Tversky, A. (1979). Prospect theory: An analysis of decision under risk. *Econometrica, 47,* 263–291.

45. Kiefe, C. I., Allison, J. J., Williams, O. D., Person, S. D., Weaver, M. T., & Weissman, N. W. (2001). Improving quality improvement using achievable benchmarks for physician feedback: A randomized controlled trial. *JAMA, 285,* 2871–2879.

46. Rogers, T., Milkman, K. L., John, L. K., & Norton, M. I. (2015) Beyond good intentions: Prompting people to make plans improves follow-through on important tasks. *Behavioral Science & Policy, 1*(2), 33–41.

editorial policy

Behavioral Science & Policy (BSP) is an international, peer-reviewed publication of the Behavioral Science & Policy Association and Brookings Institution Press. BSP features short, accessible articles describing actionable policy applications of behavioral scientific research that serves the public interest. Articles submitted to BSP undergo a dual-review process: For each article, leading disciplinary scholars review for scientific rigor and experts in relevant policy areas review for practicality and feasibility of implementation. Manuscripts that pass this dual-review are edited to ensure their accessibility to policy makers, scientists, and lay readers. BSP is not limited to a particular point of view or political ideology.

Manuscripts can be submitted in a number of different formats, each of which must clearly explain specific implications for public- and/or private-sector policy and practice.

External review of the manuscript entails evaluation by at least two outside referees—at least one in the policy arena and at least one in the disciplinary field.

Professional editors trained in BSP's style work with authors to enhance the accessibility and appeal of the material for a general audience.

Behavioral Science & Policy charges a $50 fee per submission to defray a portion of the manuscript processing costs. For the first volume of the journal, this fee has been waived.

Each of the sections below provides general information for authors about the manuscript submission process. We recommend that you take the time to read each section and review carefully the BSP Editorial Policy before submitting your manuscript to *Behavioral Science & Policy*.

Manuscript Formats
Manuscripts can be submitted in a number of different formats, each of which must clearly demonstrate the empirical basis for the article as well as explain specific implications for (public and/or private-sector) policy and practice:

- Proposals (≤ 2,500 words) specify scientifically grounded policy proposals and provide supporting evidence including concise reports of relevant studies. This category is most appropriate for describing new policy implications of previously published work or a novel policy recommendation that is supported by previously published studies.
- Findings (≤ 4,000 words) report on results of new studies and/or substantially new analysis of previously reported data sets (including formal meta-analysis) and the policy implications of the research findings. This category is most appropriate for presenting new evidence that supports a particular policy recommendation. The additional length of this format is designed to accommodate a summary of methods, results, and/or analysis of studies (though some finer details may be relegated to supplementary online materials).

- Reviews (≤ 5,000 words) survey and synthesize the key findings and policy implications of research in a specific disciplinary area or on a specific policy topic. This could take the form of describing a general-purpose behavioral tool for policy makers or a set of behaviorally grounded insights for addressing a particular policy challenge.
- Other Published Materials. BSP will sometimes solicit or accept *Essays* (≤ 5,000 words) that present a unique perspective on behavioral policy; *Letters* (≤ 500 words) that provide a forum for responses from readers and contributors, including policy makers and public figures; and *Invitations* (≤ 1,000 words with links to online Supplemental Material), which are requests from policy makers for contributions from the behavioral science community on a particular policy issue. For example, if a particular agency is facing a specific challenge and seeks input from the behavioral science community, we would welcome posting of such solicitations.

Review and Selection of Manuscripts
On submission, the manuscript author is asked to indicate the most relevant disciplinary area and policy area addressed by his/her manuscript. (In the case of some papers, a "general" policy category designation may be appropriate.) The relevant Senior Disciplinary Editor and the Senior Policy Editor provide an initial screening of the manuscripts. After initial screening, an appropriate Associate Policy Editor and Associate Disciplinary Editor serve as the stewards of each manuscript as it moves through the editorial process. The manuscript author will receive an email within approximately two weeks of submission, indicating whether the article has been sent to outside referees for further consideration. External review of the manuscript entails evaluation by at least two outside referees. In most cases, Authors will receive a response from BSP within approximately 60 days of submission. With rare exception, we will submit manuscripts to no more than two rounds of full external review. We generally do not accept re-submissions of material without an explicit invitation from an editor. Professional editors trained in the BSP style will collaborate with the author of any manuscript recommended for publication to enhance the accessibility and appeal of the material to a general audience (i.e., a broad range of behavioral scientists, public- and private-sector policy makers, and educated lay public). We anticipate no more than two rounds of feedback from the professional editors.

Standards for Novelty
BSP seeks to bring new policy recommendations and/or new evidence to the attention of public and private sector policy makers that are supported by rigorous behavioral and/or social science research. Our emphasis is on novelty of the policy application and the strength of the supporting evidence for that recommendation. We encourage submission of work based on new studies, especially field studies (for Findings and Proposals) and novel syntheses of previously published work that have a strong empirical foundation (for Reviews).

BSP will also publish novel treatments of previously published studies that focus on their significant policy implications. For instance, such a paper might involve re-working of the general emphasis, motivation, discussion of implications, and/or a re-analysis of existing data to highlight policy-relevant implications or prior work that have not been detailed elsewhere.

In our checklist for authors we ask for a brief statement that explicitly details how the present work differs from previously published work (or work under review elsewhere). When in doubt, we ask that authors include with their submission copies of related papers. Note that any text, data, or figures excerpted or paraphrased from other previously published material must clearly indicate the original source with quotation and citations as appropriate.

Authorship
Authorship implies substantial participation in research and/or composition of a manuscript. All authors must agree to the order of author listing and must have read and approved submission of the final manuscript. All authors are responsible for the accuracy and integrity of the work, and the senior author is required to have examined raw data from any studies on which the paper relies that the authors have collected.

Data Publication
BSP requires authors of accepted empirical papers to submit all relevant raw data (and, where relevant, algorithms or code for analyzing those data) and stimulus materials for publication on the journal web site so that other investigators or policymakers can verify and draw on the analysis contained in the work. In some cases, these data may be redacted slightly to protect subject anonymity and/or comply with legal restrictions. In cases where a proprietary data set is owned by a third party, a waiver to this requirement may be granted. Likewise, a waiver may be granted if a dataset is particularly complex, so that it would be impractical to post it in a sufficiently annotated form (e.g. as is sometimes the case for brain imaging data). Other waivers will be considered where appropriate. Inquiries can be directed to the BSP office.

Statement of Data Collection Procedures
BSP strongly encourages submission of empirical work that is based on multiple studies and/or a meta-analysis of several datasets. In order to protect against false positive results, we ask that authors of empirical work fully disclose relevant details concerning their data collection practices (if not in the main text then in the supplemental online materials). In particular, we ask that authors report how they determined their sample size, all data exclusions (if any), all manipulations, and all measures in the studies presented. (A template for these disclosures is included in our checklist for authors, though in some cases may be most appropriate for presentation online as Supplemental Material; for more information, see Simmons, Nelson, & Simonsohn, 2011, *Psychological Science, 22*, 1359-1366).

Copyright and License
Copyright to all published articles is held jointly by the Behavioral Science & Policy Association and Brookings Institution Press, subject to use outlined in the *Behavioral Science & Policy* publication agreement (a waiver is considered only in cases where one's employer formally and explicitly prohibits work from being copyrighted; inquiries should be directed to the BSPA office). Following publication, the manuscript author may post the accepted version of the article on his/her personal web site, and may circulate the work to colleagues and students for educational and research purposes. We also allow posting in cases where funding agencies explicitly request access to published manuscripts (e.g., NIH requires posting on PubMed Central).

Open Access
BSP posts each accepted article on our website in an open access format at least until that article has been bundled into an issue. At that point, access is granted to journal subscribers and members of the Behavioral Science & Policy Association. Questions regarding institutional constraints on open access should be directed to the editorial office.

Supplemental Material
While the basic elements of study design and analysis should be described in the main text, authors are invited to submit Supplemental Material for online publication that helps elaborate on details of research methodology and analysis of their data, as well as links to related material available online elsewhere. Supplemental material should be included to the extent that it helps readers evaluate the credibility of the contribution, elaborate on the findings presented in the paper, or provide useful guidance to policy makers wishing to act on the policy recommendations advanced in the paper. This material should be presented in as concise a manner as possible.

Embargo
Authors are free to present their work at invited colloquia and scientific meetings, but should not seek media attention for their work in advance of publication, unless the reporters in question agree to comply with BSP's press embargo. Once accepted, the paper will be considered a privileged document and only be released to the press and public when published online. BSP will strive to release work as quickly as possible, and we do not anticipate that this will create undue delays.

Conflict of Interest
Authors must disclose any financial, professional, and personal relationships that might be construed as possible sources of bias.

Use of Human Subjects
All research using human subjects must have Institutional Review Board (IRB) approval, where appropriate.